NOTES ON THE
MEDIEVAL MONASTERIES AND MINSTERS
OF ENGLAND AND WALES

WEST FRONT, CASTLE ACRE PRIORY

Medieval Monasteries and Minsters

Notes on the
Medieval Monasteries
and Minsters of England
and Wales

by

H. ERNEST ROBERTS

LONDON
S · P · C · K
1949

TO
MY WIFE

MADE IN GREAT BRITAIN

FOREWORD

IT has been my object to bring together in one book some account, though necessarily slight, of the Cathedrals, Minsters, Abbeys and Priories of England and Wales as they existed at the outbreak of war in September, 1939.

I have endeavoured to make a complete list of all the medieval establishments, from integral buildings down to slight remains; wherever, in fact, there is anything appreciable existing above ground or discernible as uncovered foundations. The various residences mentioned all incorporate portions of the original buildings, though some are much more complete than others. Nevertheless, endeavour and achievement are not necessarily synonymous terms, and there may be omissions. Therefore I have included as Appendix XII a supplementary list of all the other places where monastic establishments formerly existed, so far as I have been able to trace them; and it may be that some of these still show some fragmentary remains. Should any reader know of such sites, I should be most grateful for information regarding them.

The most convenient method of presentment seemed to be:

(a) ENGLAND, divided into counties arranged alphabetically.
(b) WALES, similarly treated.
(c) Under each county, the names of the various Orders chronologically, and grouped (1) Monks, (2) Canons, (3) Friars.

Measurements of the larger churches are given, and are internal, but exclude western towers. Areas are approximate.

Those places I have designated as " slight remains " or " vestiges ", while interesting to archaeologists, have nothing to attract the ordinary tourist.

It may be advisable to define one's terms, as names are frequently used somewhat loosely:

BENEDICTINES (Black Monks). Usually in towns. Their principal houses were Abbeys, and their subsidiaries—or " cells "—were Priories.

v

CLUNIACS (an offshoot of the Benedictines). Always Priories until later times. They owed allegiance to the Abbey of Cluny, in Burgundy.

CARTHUSIANS (a strict Order of Monks). Always Priories, sometimes called Charterhouses.

CISTERCIANS (White Monks). Invariably in remote places. Monasteries are always Abbeys, and Nunneries are Priories.

SECULAR CANONS (non-monastic). Their great churches were Minsters, and only such are dealt with in this book. In addition, they had a large number of Collegiate Churches, though these come more within the category of Parish Churches.

AUGUSTINIANS (Black Canons Regular). Their houses were generally Priories, though Dorchester, Thornton and others were Abbeys. A few Priories, such as Bourne and Bruton, became Abbeys shortly before the Dissolution.

GILBERTINES (an English Order). Always Priories.

PREMONSTRATENSIANS (White Canons Regular). Always Abbeys, in remote places. They owed allegiance to the Abbey of Premontre.

CATHEDRALS. Canterbury, Durham, Ely, Norwich, Rochester, Winchester and Worcester were served by Benedictines under a Prior.

Carlisle was served by a Priory of Augustinian Canons.

The Minsters (York, Beverley, Lincoln, etc.) were served by a Chapter of Secular Canons—usually under a Dean.

Since the Dissolution the following churches have been raised to Cathedral status :

ABBEYS *Benedictine* Chester, Gloucester, Peterborough and St. Albans.

Augustinian Bristol.

PRIORIES *Augustinian* Oxford, Portsmouth and Southwark.

MINSTERS *Secular*   Ripon and Southwell.

While most of these notes are the result of careful personal study extending over very many years, my thanks are due to my friend, Mr. Thomas P. Bell of West Kirby, for information regarding approximately forty of the lesser establishments visited

by him, which I have been unable to reach; also to many
parochial clergy for their kindly interest and help in connection
with churches under their control.

A list of works consulted would be too large to enumerate,
though my indebtedness to such works of reference as the various
County Directories, the " Little Guides ", sundry monographs
and other publications, is gratefully acknowledged.

H. ERNEST ROBERTS

" *Ardenholme* "
   West Kirby, Cheshire.
      May, 1947

CONTENTS

CONTENTS

LIST OF ILLUSTRATIONS

xi

The arrangement set out above is approximately the order in which one would see the various subjects if one were to enter by the gateway, cross the court to the church, visit the church, go round the cloister and finally the outer court.

Acknowledgment is made to the following for permission to use the photographs in this book :—

Facing page

Aero-films, Ltd. . . . 16 (1)
G. C. Culmer . . . 36 (bottom)
The Dean of Chester . . 100
Frith and Co. . . . 77 (bottom)
Ernest C. Garnett . . . 28, 29 (top), 44 (bottom), 76 (bottom), 77 (top), 116, 117
E. Chambré Hardman, F.R.P.S. 68 (top), 85
A. F. Kersting, F.R.P.S. . . 16 (4), 60, 92 (bottom), 93, 109 (bottom)
H.M. Ministry of Works . . 108 (top)
The National Buildings Record . 16 (3 & 6), 36 (top), 52
Walter Scott of Bradford . 84 (bottom), 92 (top), 101 (top)
Henry C. Stacy, A.R.P.S. . *Frontispiece*, 16 (2, 7 & 8), 45, 53, 68 (bottom), 69, 76 (top), 101 (bottom)
Valentine of Dundee . 16 (5), 29 (bottom), 61, 108 (bottom)
Reece Winstone, A.R.P.S. . 37, 44 (top), 84 (top), 109 (top)

MONKS, CANONS AND FRIARS

I

Monks, Canons and Friars

ORDERS OF MONKS

Benedictines. In the early centuries of the Christian era, men who wished to retire from the world and lead a contemplative life either lived alone as hermits or with others of like mind as cenobites. But although cenobites lived in groups or settlements, there was no common rule of life to bind them together in genuine communities as the term came to be understood later. It was not until the end of the 5th century that St. Benedict, himself a hermit, conceived the idea of bringing together a group of such men and welding them together under a definite Rule, over which he presided. On this basis the Order of Monks known as Benedictine was founded.

Each community of these monks was an independent body, living under its own abbot, and owing allegiance to no central authority. Their day was divided between a regular series of services, contemplation, study, and the necessary work of the convent. The first service of the day was at 2 a.m., when Matins was sung; this was followed by Lauds at 4.30 a.m.; Prime at 6 a.m.; Terce at 9 a.m.; Sext at noon; Nones at 3 p.m.; Vespers at 4.30 p.m.; and Compline at 6 p.m. As time went on Matins and Lauds were taken together at midnight, and there was a tendency to join other services. Mass was sung during the forenoon on Sundays in early times, but daily later.

With the growth of the Order in numbers and influence, it became the custom for servants to be employed to do the necessary manual work, and for the monks to confine themselves to the services, contemplation and such work as the illumination and writing of books, the making of vestments and other requirements of the services of the Church.

As with all human institutions, abuses and slackness crept in,

3

and various reforms were effected from time to time, until in 910 the first great reform was initiated.

Cluniacs. In that year the Abbey of Cluny was founded, and became under successive abbots the centre of a widespread reform, involving the foundation of a new Order. The principal difference in organisation was that the parent Abbey of Cluny was the only abbey, all the daughter houses spread over Europe being priories, and all owing allegiance to Cluny. This Order became extremely powerful and wealthy, and its buildings and services very ornate. Its early spirituality tended to become submerged, so much so that the desire for a return to a simpler form of monasticism asserted itself.

Carthusians. The outcome was the founding of a new Order at Grande-Chartreuse by St. Bruno in 1086. In this Order there was something in the nature of a return to the old hermit form. The monks did not live, sleep and eat together in a common cloister, dormitory and refectory, but each had his own cell with a little plot of land for growing herbs, etc. These cells were grouped round the cloister, and were so arranged that each monk's meals were passed to him through an opening constructed on an angle, so that no visible or other communication took place between the monk in his cell and the monk delivering the meal. The only occasions on which they came together were for the services in the Church. Although this Order spread throughout Europe, the strictness of its rule prevented it from being a popular Order, and also saved it from the decadence which overtook other Orders. It maintained itself strongly throughout the Middle Ages, though not in the large numbers of most of the others. There were only nine of their houses in England, and of these only Mount Grace in Yorkshire still retains sufficient evidence of its lay-out to enable a clear idea of their mode of life to be formed.

Cistercians. Soon after the establishment of the Carthusians, other monks, who wished for a less strict reform, and one more in accord with the original Rule of St. Benedict, made various tentative efforts in that direction. The best of these, and the only one that survived, was founded in 1098 at the Abbey of Citeaux. At first progress was slow, but under the joint efforts of St. Stephen Harding (an Englishman), who was the second

Abbot of Citeaux, and St. Bernard, Abbot of the daughter house
of Clairvaux, the new Order made great strides. In this Order
all daughter houses were called Abbeys, and each was ruled
by its own abbot; but, unlike the original Benedictines, each
abbot owed allegiance to the Mother Abbey of Citeaux. They
lived in community like the Benedictines and Cluniacs, but were
extremely Puritanic in their outlook. Their buildings were
severe, permitting no ornament of any kind, no sculptures, no
silk vestments (only plain material), no gold or silver vessels,
but usually pewter. They avoided towns, and built their abbeys
in remote places; places which to-day look very attractive, but
which in the 12th century were wild and bleak. This remoteness
necessitated a special group of men in each abbey to do the
manual work, since servants were not available. The need was
met by lay brothers, or conversi, who took the usual monastic
vows, but were illiterate. They lived in the west range; their
common room and refectory were on the ground floor, with
dormitory over, and they had the Nave for their services. They
performed all the manual work: repairs, farm labouring, metal-
smelting and such like. In later times, when the abbeys became
wealthy, most of the original rigour was lost; the lay brothers
gave place to paid servants, towers were built, ornamentation
and a more lavish ritual began to appear, and the worldliness
which beset so many monasteries (with the exception of the
Carthusians) made itself manifest, though on the whole to a less
extent than among the monasteries in the cities and large towns.
We owe a great debt to the Cistercians, for it was they who in
the first instance developed our sheep-farming, iron-smelting
and other industries.

General. In the early days of monasticism monks were
generally laymen, with only sufficient priests among them to
maintain the services at their proper level. Later the proportion
of priests increased, and the enlargement of choirs and other
places for altars, at which each could say his daily Mass, is apparent
in almost every abbey church.

The first Benedictine House in England was established by
St. Augustine at Canterbury; the first Carthusian at Witham
(Somerset); and the first Cistercian at Waverley (Surrey).

ORDERS OF CANONS

Seculars. For the first thousand years, with the exception of such comparatively few priests as became monks, the clergy were seculars; i.e., they lived in the world, and worked among the ordinary people much as they do now. There were, however, large churches, such as cathedrals and collegiate churches, where a body of seculars were responsible for the services. These bodies are the chapters of cathedrals, and the " colleges " of the collegiate churches. They did not live in community, but each had one or more " prebends " or livings, for whose ministrations he was responsible. The cathedral services were taken by such canons in turn, and their periods of residence were decided by the chapter as a whole. There were four permanent members of each chapter : the Dean (or President of the Chapter), the Chancellor, the Precentor and the Treasurer. Each canon had his own seat in choir, usually marked with the name of his prebend. This system, with inevitable modifications brought about by changing times and conditions, continues in its main features to the present day.

Augustinians. The idea of a common life, based on that of monks, appealed to a number of the clergy, and several attempts were made to adapt the monastic system to priests who had their parochial duties to perform. About the middle of the 11th century an Order of canons came into being who lived in community and followed a Rule extracted from the writings of St. Augustine of Hippo, from which their name of Augustinians was derived. They seem to have worked the parishes in the neighbourhood of their priories, but at home they lived very much as the monks lived. They had a common dormitory and refectory, chapter house, infirmary and so forth, built on a similar plan to those of the monastic Orders proper. Generally their houses were priories, but there were some abbeys, though the terms have no relative significance. Great houses like Bridlington and Cartmel were priories, while some lesser ones, such as Lilleshall, were abbeys. Each house, however, was independent, like the Benedictines. They settled in all manner of places : large cities, small towns, and even remote districts such as the Cistercians favoured. In later times they approximated more and more closely to the monasteries proper, particularly when the proportion of priests in the latter increased. Their first house in England was St. Botolph's Priory, Colchester.

Premonstratensians. This Order was founded by St. Norbert of Premontre, near Laon, about the beginning of the 12th century. They performed no parochial duties, but were modelled on the Cistercians, living in remote places. Their habit, like that of the Cistercians, was white. Their houses were all abbeys, and each owed allegiance to the Mother Abbey of Premontre. They were not a wealthy Order, and their establishments are not specially impressive.

Gilbertine. This was exclusively an English Order, founded by St. Gilbert of Sempringham in the 12th century. He strove to combine a house of canons, following the Augustinian Rule, with a house of nuns, following the Cistercian Rule. There was no communication between the two, except the church; and even there a wall divided the canons from the nuns, so that neither could see the other. The men lived in the usual suite of buildings on one side of the church, and the women similarly on the other. Many Gilbertine establishments, however, were for one sex only. Most of the houses of this Order were in the eastern counties, and the only church still in use is that at Old Malton, Yorks. This, however, was not a "double" house, and the existing church is little more than a fragment, albeit a beautiful one. Their largest house was at Watton, Yorks, where the Prior's House is still a residence, though all else except foundations has disappeared.

ORDERS OF FRIARS

Although they lived in community and took the triple vow of poverty, chastity and obedience, like monks and canons regular, friars lived quite a different sort of life. Their houses were primarily headquarters from which they worked. They were mendicants, living on alms and wandering about the country, using as a base any house of their own order which happened to be convenient. Their principal object was to reach the outcast and poor, and their method was preaching. Generally speaking, the friaries were in towns, and most towns of any size had houses of the four principal Orders. Their churches were specially designed for large congregations, the naves being wide and spacious, with slender piers so as not to impede the preacher's voice.

Franciscans. The earliest Order of Friars was founded by St. Francis of Assisi in 1210. Their first settlement in this country was at Canterbury in 1224. They were known as " Grey Friars ", from the colour of their habit.

Dominicans. This Order was founded by St. Dominic in 1216, and was known as the " Black Friars ". In addition to their normal duties they had scholastic interests, and founded houses both at Oxford and Cambridge which became celebrated centres of learning. They settled first at Oxford in 1221.

Carmelites. Next came the Carmelites, or White Friars. Their choice of sites for their houses was not invariably in the towns, for, like the White Monks (Cistercians) and White Canons (Premonstratensians), they sometimes built in remote places. This circumstance has resulted in the ruined, but tolerably perfect, Hulne Friary being still in existence for the study of this type of religious house. It stands in Alnwick Park, the seat of the Duke of Northumberland, in beautiful surroundings. Their first English house was established in 1240 at Aylesford (Kent).

Austin Friars. This Order was formed by the amalgamation of a number of lesser bodies, and, like the Franciscans and Dominicans, was confined to cities and towns. They wore black habits. Their first foundation was at Clare (Suffolk), c. 1230.

General. From the fact that friaries were in towns, and their work non-parochial, they were not popular with the ordinary clergy. When they were dissolved their establishments were no longer required for Church purposes, and either disappeared altogether, or were converted to secular uses, as will be seen from the notes on the individual buildings or ruins that remain. The streets or districts in which they were established are often called after them, so that one meets with " Blackfriars ", " Greyfriars " and " Whitefriars " in many towns, where such names are all that is left to mark their former presence.

II

The Parts of a Monastery

In the nature of things (such as site, or the position of the monastery relative to a town or a river, or the individual peculiarities of different Orders, and so forth), there are no two conventual establishments with precisely the same plan. There is, nevertheless, a definite general scheme followed essentially by all Orders except the Carthusian. In the latter instance there are marked divergencies, as has been pointed out in the chapter on the various Orders.

No one example remains of a complete set of buildings still standing, but at many of the ruined Cistercian abbeys—e.g., Fountains, Kirkstall and Rievaulx—there are very extensive remains, and where any building has been destroyed to the ground the foundations are exposed so as to show the plan. To a lesser extent the same may be said of Furness, Tintern and others.

Of churches still in use, many of the outer buildings are to be seen at Canterbury and Gloucester, though in altered form. The inner buildings surrounding the cloister also partially remain at those two cathedrals, and at Durham, Westminster and Worcester. But the most complete set of the inner, or cloister, buildings is to be seen at Chester, and it will therefore be convenient to take them as typical.

It is scarcely necessary to state that by far the most important building in every monastery was the church, which was the essence of the convent's existence. It dominated the whole plan of the place, and in important abbeys was generally a building of considerable magnitude and architectural splendour. The normal plan was cruciform—i.e., in the form of a cross having four arms : the choir and presbytery to the east, the nave to the west, and a north and south transept. Where these four arms intersected rose the great central tower. If we take Chester as our example, we are confronted with an unusual transept scheme, for the south is the largest in the country, consisting of four bays, whereas the north is small. The normal scheme is for the two transepts to balance one another. The reason for this

PLAN OF CHESTER CATHEDRAL

(1) Choir
(2) Nave
(3) North Transept
(4) South Transept
(5) Crossing
(6) Lady Chapel
(7) Sacristy
(8) Consistory Court
(9) Outer Court
(10) Cloister Walks
(11) Vestibule
(12) Chapter House
(13) Slype
(14) Daystair
(15) Parlour
(16) Refectory
(17) Reader's Pulpit
(18) Site of Kitchen
(19) Cellarium
(20) Garth

PLAN OF CHESTER CATHEDRAL

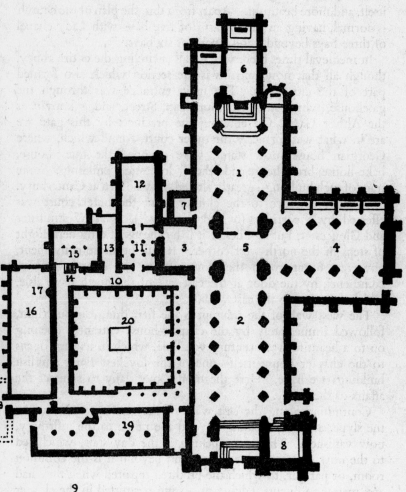

divergence at Chester is that the cloister buildings abut on the north, thus making extension or enlargement in that direction impracticable.   When enlargement became necessary to provide more accommodation for altars, it was therefore entirely effected on the south, and that transept is almost as large as the nave itself, and more beautiful.   Apart from this, the plan of the church is normal, having an eastern arm of five bays with Lady chapel of three bays beyond; and a nave of six bays.

In medieval times there was a wall encircling the entire abbey, though all that now remains is the section which also formed part of the city walls.   The main entrance was through the gatehouse, which stands in Northgate Street, and is known as the Abbey Gate.   On entering the precincts by this gate we are in what was formerly the outer court, round which, where Georgian houses now stand, were grouped the guest-house, bake-house, brew-house and other " domestic " buildings.   Some trace of such buildings, greatly altered, may be seen at Canterbury.

Usually, entrance to the cloister from the outer court was effected by a corridor (or " dark-entry "), as at Westminster and Gloucester, but at Chester it is by means of a modern flight of steps in the north-west corner.   It will be more convenient, however, to approach the cloister from the church, and to commence by the door at the east end of the north nave aisle, which opens on to the east walk.

The west wall of the transept is the first thing on our right, followed immediately by the chapter-house entrance, opening on to a beautiful 13th-century vestibule, which in its turn opens to the chapter house itself—one of the loveliest Early English buildings we have.   Here the monks met daily to transact the affairs of the abbey.

Continuing along the east walk of the cloister, we come to the slype, a passage leading beyond the range to the infirmary, now vanished.   The next opening is the day stair, which led to the now destroyed dormitory, and beyond it is the common room, or parlour, to which the brethren repaired when they had any matter to discuss, talking not being permitted in the cloister itself.   The dormitory formerly occupied the floor over this range of buildings, but nothing of it is left.

We now turn along the North Walk, and on the right is the lavatory where the monks washed their hands before going into the refectory for meals. The door on the right leads into the refectory, a noble apartment which has been greatly improved recently by the addition of a splendid hammer-beam roof. Here the monks took their meals, during which one of their number would read passages from Holy Writ, or from the Fathers of the Church. The reader's pulpit still remains, and is the only one left except for that at Beaulieu Abbey refectory, which is now the parish church there. Adjoining the refectory to the west is a corridor which formerly led to the kitchen.

The West Walk is occupied by the cellarium, in which were stored the provisions necessary for the monks, servants, guests, etc. Over this undercroft formerly stood the abbot's house, as is still the case at Gloucester. Note on the opposite side the bays in the southern half of the " screen " between the walk and the garth. These were for study and writing. They continue along the entire south walk, which abuts against the nave.

The square formed by these four walks is the Garth, with the main reservoir of the abbey in the centre. There is now a fountain in the midst of it. This was not the monks' cemetery, as is sometimes suggested. That appurtenance lay to the south-east of the church, in the neighbourhood of the infirmary.

Although at Chester, as at Canterbury and Gloucester, the conventual buildings are to the north of the church, it was more usual to have them on the south, as at Durham, Westminster, Worcester, Norwich and scores of others—an arrangement which enabled the inmates to take full advantage of the sun.

The arrangements set out above, though normal for Benedictine and Augustinian houses, differ in some particulars from those of Cistercians. The main points of divergence in the case of the latter arose from the necessity of providing for the lay brothers, or conversi. This was done in the West Range, where, in place of the abbot's house, a long, two-storied building served as their quarters; the ground floor containing their refectory and common room, while the floor above was their dormitory. This scheme is still plainly in evidence at Fountains.

Another variant was the siting of the refectory. This was on the walk opposite to the church, as in Benedictine and other houses, but instead of running east to west, as they do, the Cistercian axis is north to south. In later days, when lay brothers were abolished, the West Range was converted into quarters for the abbot or prior, and in some cases the position of the refectory was altered, as may be seen at Cleeve in Somerset. Here the existing late refectory runs east to west, and the foundations of the original north to south building may be traced.

In all abbey and priory churches the choir, presbytery and transepts were reserved exclusively for the monks or canons, as the case might be. But the use of the nave varied with the Order. Very frequently in Benedictine and Augustinian churches the nave was used as the parish church, the parish altar being placed against the rood screen—a stone structure which extended across the width of the nave and divided the convent from the parish, as may be seen at St. Albans. This use of the nave is the reason why so many naves remain in use to this day, where everything to the east of the rood screen has perished.

In Cistercian abbeys, where there were lay brothers but no parish, the nave was appropriated to their use, though the nave aisles continued to be used by the regular monks. In a large number of instances a wall was built connecting the piers, so that the processions of the regulars should not disturb or be disturbed by the services of the lay brothers. Remains of such walls may be seen at Tintern and Buildwas, to mention two examples where they are conspicuous.

APPROXIMATE DATES OF THE VARIOUS
STYLES OF ARCHITECTURE

NORMAN (Nor.)	William I, II and Henry I	1066–1135
LATE NORMAN and TRANSITIONAL (Tr.)	Stephen, Henry II and Richard I	1135–1199
EARLY ENGLISH (E.E.) and GEOMETRIC	John and Henry III	1199–1272
DECORATED (Dec.)	Edward I, II and Edward III	1272–1350
PERPENDICULAR (Perp.)	Edward III Richard II Henry IV, V and VI Edward IV Richard III	1350–1485
TUDOR	Henry VII and Henry VIII	1485–1547

CHESTER CATHEDRAL FROM THE AIR.

Facing page 16.

NORMAN STYLE—ROMSEY ABBEY.

TRANSITIONAL STYLE—DEEPING ST. JAMES PRIORY

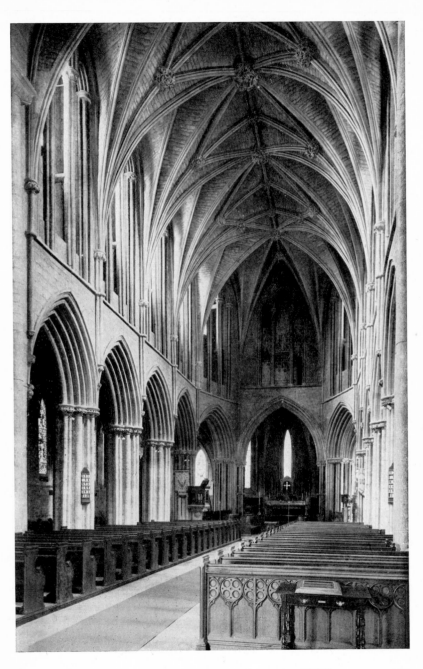

EARLY ENGLISH STYLE—PERSHORE ABBEY.

GEOMETRIC STYLE—BRIDLINGTON PRIORY.

DECORATED STYLE—BEVERLEY MINSTER

PERPENDICULAR STYLE—CANTERBURY CATHEDRAL.

TUDOR STYLE—BATH ABBEY.

Facing page 17.

PROVINCES OF CANTERBURY AND YORK

Bedfordshire

Monks

Benedictine

ELSTOW ABBEY (Nuns). Clerestoried nave with aisles still in use; Norman and E.E. The Norman piers are square, the E.E. shafted and octagonal. The vestry is an E.E. vaulted chamber with a central column of Purbeck marble, at the north-west corner of the church. It is the most attractive feature of the building. West front E.E. in lower stage, with doorway—very much restored; upper part Perp. There is a fine detached north-west tower (Norman and Perp.) with a small spire.

The central tower, transepts, choir and conventual buildings were destroyed.

Cistercian

WARDON ABBEY. Some refectory windows and a chimney are incorporated in a house.

Canons

Augustinian

BUSHMEAD PRIORY. Residence. Portions of the monastic buildings are incorporated in the house, notably the refectory.

DUNSTABLE PRIORY. The six western bays of the Norman nave, with two aisles and triforium—but no clerestory—form the parish church. The piers on either side are compound, with a Perp. north aisle and modern south aisle rebuilt in Norman style. The original clerestory was removed in the 15th century, and the triforium openings adapted as a clerestory. The rood screen forms the base of the present east wall.

The beautiful west front is Norman and E.E., with a Norman doorway of four orders enclosing a smaller Perp. doorway. The tower (N.W.) is E.E.

This is a very fine building.

The length of the church is 120 feet.

The choir, transepts, central tower and conventual buildings were demolished, though remains of the gateway may still be seen.

NEWENHAM PRIORY.   A ruined wall is the only relic.

Gilbertine

CHICKSANDS PRIORY.   Residence. The double cloisters for Canons and Nuns are incorporated in the house, the south and east fronts of which were rebuilt by Wyatt.

Friars

Franciscan

BEDFORD.   The cloisters and refectory form part of a house.

Berkshire

Monks

Benedictine

ABINGDON ABBEY (Mitred).   The church and most of the buildings have disappeared, but the 15th-century gatehouse remains, also two buildings which may have been the prior's house and the guest house. The prior's house has some good E.E. and Dec. features, with a fine 13th-century hooded chimney. The guest house is Perp.

HURLEY PRIORY (c. Westminster).   The church, a small, unaisled Saxon and Norman building of flint and chalk, with a Norman west front, is the parish church. It consists of chancel and nave, with some mid-19th-century restorations in "Norman" style. Some portions of the conventual buildings may still be seen, notably the refectory (Norman and Dec.), with scanty remains of the east and west ranges.

The priory dovecot is close by, and two barns.

READING ABBEY (Mitred).   Ruin. Remains of the church, chapter house, dormitory, rere-dorter, refectory and gatehouse. Very little masonry is left, chiefly rubble.

It was a Norman church.

Canons

Augustinian

BISHAM PRIORY. Residence (Tudor), known as Bisham Abbey. It incorporates the 14th-century refectory, an octagonal tower, and the parlour. The barn also remains.

POUGHLEY PRIORY. The kitchen and dormitory form part of a private house.

Friars

Franciscan

READING. The Grey Friars' Church has passed through many vicissitudes, but happily its nave is once again used as a church, though it has no chancel.

It has been in turn :—

1543–1560, Reading Town Hall.
1560–1613, workhouse.
1613–1863, gaol.

The rehabilitation of the nave in 1863 has been followed by a new north transept and a restoration of the south transept, some part of the latter being old work.

Buckingham

Monks

Benedictine

ANKERWYCKE PRIORY (Nuns). Slight remains.

BRADWELL PRIORY. Some remains of the chapel (E.E.) are incorporated in a farm building.

LUFFIELD PRIORY. Foundations and fish-ponds.

LITTLE MARLOW PRIORY (Nuns). Foundations.

Canons

Augustinian

BURNHAM PRIORY (Nuns). The present nunnery incorporates the east range with sacristy, chapter house, parlour and warming-room. There is also a wall of the refectory and portions of the infirmary. Generally E.E. of a plain and simple character.

CHETWODE PRIORY. The chancel and north chapel of the priory church are in use as the parish church, having become so in 1480. The priory was dissolved in 1460, owing to its poverty.

The chancel is E.E., and has a beautiful E.E. sedilia with foliated capitals on the south side.

The east window is of five lancets; the north and south windows are triple lancets, the south retaining its original glass.

The chapel is Dec. (c. 1330).

There is a low 15th-century tower at the north-west corner. The nave and transepts were destroyed.

This is a very attractive example of the E.E. style internally, though unpretentious externally.

There are no other remains.

NOTLEY ABBEY. There is a barn with an E.E. corbel table. The west range is converted into a residence.

Cambridgeshire

Monks

Benedictine

CHATTERIS PRIORY (Nuns). Remains are very scanty.

ST. RADEGUND'S PRIORY, CAMBRIDGE (Nuns). At the close of the 15th century (1497) this nunnery was suppressed, and converted into Jesus College, Cambridge. In adapting the nunnery buildings to the purposes of a college, much alteration was necessary and unavoidable. Of the church, the choir became the College chapel, with the transepts as ante-chapel, while the eastern bay of the nave houses the organ. The central tower, a somewhat plain one, still stands. Modern alterations comprise the lancets in the east wall (which replace a Perp. window), and the roof (the former one having been of low pitch).

The nave has lost both its aisles, and the greater part of it, together with the prioress's house, was converted into the Master's Lodge and some chambers.

What remains of the cloister buildings are the chapter house entrance (chapter house itself destroyed); common room; refectory (College hall); and guest house (library). The garth is enlarged by the width of the demolished nave aisle.

DENNY PRIORY (Nuns). Remains include portions of the refectory (Dec.), and a considerable part of the church (Norman). The priory changed ownership several times, and at the Dissolution belonged to the Order of St. Clare.

ELY CATHEDRAL. One of the largest of the cathedrals, with several unusual features. The crossing is an octagon (Dec.); a unique and very beautiful structure, with an octagonal lantern. At the west end there is a lovely E.E. porch, but only one tower, the lowest stages of which are Norman work, the middle stages E.E., and the octagon at the top Perp. A fine Norman and E.E. transept lies to the south of this tower, but there is no corresponding one on the north. If there ever was one, it has been demolished.

The Lady chapel (Dec.) occupies a position to the north-east of the transept, and is a large and beautiful one. Its wonderful carvings are sadly mutilated.

The nave is Norman, with compound piers, in the usual three stories. The choir is Dec., and the presbytery E.E.—both among the best examples of their periods.

The chapter house, refectory, cloisters and other buildings were destroyed by the Puritans during the Civil War, and have not been rebuilt. A small part of the cloister remains, and also of the infirmary. The latter now forms part of some houses, and some Norman arches are to be seen.

The principal periods are:

NORMAN
Nave and transepts.
Lowest stages of tower.
St. Catherine's Chapel (a modern restoration in Norman style).

EARLY ENGLISH
Presbytery and retro-choir.
Galilee porch (west end).
Middle stages of tower.

DECORATED
The octagon and choir.
Lady chapel.

PERPENDICULAR
Highest stage of tower.
Two eastern chantry chapels. Windows.

17TH CENTURY
Part of north transept.

19TH CENTURY
Reredos (Gilbert Scott).

The choir and presbytery are vaulted; the nave has a painted wooden ceiling; transept has a hammer-beam roof.

Total length	517 feet.
Length from tower arch to east window	445 „
Length of nave	230 „
Height of nave	86 „
Width of nave	78 „
Transept	180 „
Diameter of octagon	74 „
Height of western tower . . .	215 „
Area	46,000 sq. feet.

ICKLETON PRIORY (Nuns). Scanty.

ISLEHAM PRIORY (Alien). The small Late Norman church is, or was, used as a barn.

THORNEY ABBEY (Mitred). The greater part of the church, including choir and transepts, was dismantled shortly after the Dissolution. The nave aisles were removed in 1636. The present church retains five bays of the nave of the abbey church, with compound Norman piers having large vaulting shafts. The arches are filled in with walling having Perp. windows inset. The former triforium now serves as clerestory, with Perp. windows set in the Norman arches; the original clerestory has gone. The west front is Norman and Perp., with two Perp. turrets. West doorway dated 1638. The original Perp. window is walled up, with a smaller one inset.

The present transepts were erected in 1840–1 by Blore. There is no rebuilding east of this.

Apart from the church, only some foundations remain.

Canons

Augustinian

ANGLESEY PRIORY. The residence called Anglesey Abbey incorporates a 13th-century vaulted chamber, possibly the parlour, which is used as a dining-room.

Cheshire

Monks

Benedictine

BIRKENHEAD PRIORY (c. Chester). Portions of the prior's house and church remain, and the undercroft of the refectory. The chapter house is used as a chapel, belonging to the adjoining parish church; it is vaulted and mainly Norman, though partly Perp. It served as Birkenhead Parish Church for about three centuries after the Dissolution.

CHESTER CATHEDRAL. There are good examples of all styles, a specially noteworthy feature being the Dec. south transept, the largest in England, and a very beautiful one. It is in four bays, is double-aisled, and has a fine south window.

The choir is late E.E.; the nave Dec. and Perp. The north transept is small, and has a fine old Norman arch on its east side.

The claustral buildings are exceptionally complete, comprising the cloister itself, with chapter house and vestibule, slype, daystair, parlour, refectory, undercroft of abbot's house, and the abbey gate.

It was an abbey until the Dissolution, when it became one of the cathedrals of the New Foundation.

The principal building styles are:

NORMAN
    North transept.
    North wall of nave.
    Part of north-west tower base.

EARLY ENGLISH
    Choir.
    Lady chapel.
    Part of north choir aisle.
    Chapter house and vestibule.
    Refectory.

DECORATED
    South transept.
    South aisle windows.
    Nave arcades.
    Abbey gate.

C

PERPENDICULAR Clerestory.
East end of north choir aisle.
Tower.
West window and front.
Cloisters.
South porch.
Various windows.

1689–1707 Choir re-cased.

19TH CENTURY Vaults—nave in oak (lierne).
Reredos (Salviati).

The cathedral is vaulted throughout.

Total length	355 feet.
West wall to east window	280 ,,
Length of nave	145 ,,
Height of nave	78 ,,
Width of nave	75 ,,
Across transept	185 ,,
Height of tower	127 ,,
Area	32,220 sq. feet.

Cistercian

COMBERMERE ABBEY. This is a seat, containing some small portions of the original buildings. It is not open to visitors.

Canons

Seculars

ST. JOHN'S CHURCH. In the early 12th century this was the cathedral church of Chester.

Most of the eastern limb, also the western tower, are picturesque ruins.

The present church consists of four bays of the nave (having massive Norman cylindrical columns with scalloped capitals, E.E. triforium and clerestory), the crossing, and one bay of the Norman choir. East and west walls are modern.

The chapter house (E.E.) is a rectangle, and has only recently been cleared and restored to use. It is vaulted, and has a central pier.

Augustinian

NORTON PRIORY. A few remains, chiefly a crypt and a Norman doorway.

Cornwall

Monks

Benedictine

ST. MICHAEL'S MOUNT. The small aisleless chapel (70 feet by 20 feet) of this alien priory is still in existence, with Norman, Dec. and Perp. features. The refectory and other parts are included in the house.

TINTAGEL PRIORY. Belonging to the vicarage is an old gateway, and another building said to have formed part of an alien Nunnery.

Canons

Augustinian

BODMIN PRIORY. Only a few carved stones now remain.

LAUNCESTON PRIORY. A Norman doorway is the sole remnant.

ST. GERMANS PRIORY. The nave is still the parish church. It consists of six bays, the north arcade being Transitional with cylindrical piers, the south mainly Perp., but retaining two Norman piers. The south aisle itself is Perp., the north rebuilt in 1802. The Perp. east window seems to have been moved from the former east wall when the chancel fell in 1592.

There is a Dec. chapel.

The west front has a Norman doorway flanked by two towers, the lower stages of which are also Norman. The upper part of the north-west tower is octagonal.

There are no other remains, unless the adjoining residence incorporates any. The church stands in private grounds.

Cumberland

Monks

Benedictine

ST. BEES PRIORY (c. St. Mary's, York).   A plain, cruciform church
with a tower and low spire over the crossing.   The nave of six
bays with clerestory, and one bay of the choir, form the parish
church.   The rest of the choir (Transitional) is separated from the
church, and, much mutilated, is used as a Parish Room.   The
church is mostly E.E., with a Norman west door.   The tower
above the roof line is modern (Butterfield).   Nothing else left.

SEATON PRIORY (Nuns).   Scanty.

WETHERAL PRIORY.   Gatehouse only.

Cistercian

CALDER ABBEY.   A small but beautiful ruin, mainly E.E.   A fair
portion of the church remains, together with the chapter house.
A residence occupies the site of the refectory, etc.

HULME CULTRAM ABBEY.   The present parish church consists of
six bays of the nave (Transitional) of the abbey church, with neither
aisles nor clerestory.   Both arcades are walled up.   The base of a
former western tower serves as a porch (Perp.).   No other remains,
apart from stones re-used in later buildings.

Canons

Augustinian

CARLISLE CATHEDRAL.   Only two bays of the nave remain
(Norman).   The building consists chiefly of choir and transepts,
with a Perp. tower over the crossing.   The choir has fine Dec.
piers, with beautifully sculptured capitals, and there are some E.E.
features, notably the mouldings of the arches.   The east window
is the largest and finest Dec. window in England; the glass in the
tracery is ancient, while that in the lights is modern.   The refectory
is now used as the chapter house, and for other meetings, and there
are some fragments of the original chapter house in the churchyard.
The prior's house, enlarged, is now the Deanery.

The different styles are:

GATEWAY—COLCHESTER ABBEY.

Facing page 28.

GATEHOUSE—ST. OSYTH'S PRIORY.

HOSPITIUM—MONTACUTE PRIORY.

Facing page 29.

NORMAN   Nave and south transept.

EARLY ENGLISH   St. Catherine's Chapel.
                The mouldings of the choir arches.

DECORATED   Choir and vault (barrel).

PERPENDICULAR   Upper part of tower.

Principal dimensions:

Total length	212	feet.
Length of nave	39	,,
Height of nave	65	,,
Width of nave	60	,,
Across transept	110	,,
Length of choir	134	,,
Height of choir	72	,,
Width of choir	72	,,
Height of tower	112	,,
Area	15,730	sq. feet.

LANERCOST PRIORY. The E.E. nave (with a rather ugly east wall built in the west arch of the former central tower) and north aisle form the parish church. An attractive arcaded clerestory runs all round, except on the east. The E.E. west front is very good.

The crossing, eastern arm, transepts and undercroft of refectory (all E.E.) constitute a well-preserved ruin in charge of the Office of Works. Refectory and chapter house have gone.

The western range is used for parish purposes, and the vicarage includes portions of the guest house.

The outer arch of the gateway still stands.

Derbyshire

Canons

Augustinian

CHURCH GRESLEY PRIORY. The parish church, as it now stands, is to a considerable extent a modern building, but the two Dec. arches (chamfered), which spring from an octagonal pier and divide the nave from its single aisle, are a relic of the priory church, together with the Perp. tower, which is unusually placed at the east end of the north aisle.

There are no other remains.

REPTON PRIORY. The west range of the cloister (guest hall and prior's lodging), a 13th-century gateway and some walls, and the cloister garth, are included in the school. The foundations of the church are also exposed.

Premonstratensian

BEAUCHIEF ABBEY. Slight remains only, chiefly the lower portion of western tower (E.E.), portions of nave, and gatehouse. The ruins belong to Sheffield Corporation.

DALE ABBEY. Only the outline of the east window and the foundations of part of the church are left.

Devon

Monks

Benedictine

EXETER ST. CATHERINE'S (Nuns). Slight remains.

EXETER: ST. NICHOLAS' PRIORY. Nothing left of the church, cloister, chapter house or dormitory. The west range, restored, comprising a Norman crypt, kitchen, a Perp. tower, prior's lodgings and guest hall (E.E., Dec. and Perp.), are the property of the Corporation. The refectory and its undercroft are in private ownership.

PILTON PRIORY, BARNSTAPLE (c. Malmesbury). The church continues in use as the parish church, and consists of chancel, with south chapel, nave with aisles (E.E. and Perp.) and south porch. It is a three-gable building, with no clerestory. The tower stands at the east end of the north aisle, to the north of the chancel, and was rebuilt in a somewhat severe style in 1696. No other remains.

TAVISTOCK ABBEY (Mitred). Some portions are incorporated in the Bedford Hotel, and there is a well-restored Perp. gatehouse. The refectory, much altered, serves as a Unitarian chapel.

TOTNES PRIORY. Ruin; chiefly refectory, precinct wall, abbot's gate and a fine Perp. gatehouse.

Cluniac

BARNSTAPLE PRIORY. The remains are very meagre, and are incorporated in some cottages. They are chiefly portions of the chancel.

Cistercian

BUCKFAST ABBEY. Some slight remnants of the old place exist, but the abbey is now rebuilt, and in Roman Catholic hands.

BUCKLAND ABBEY. Residence; a conversion of the church itself.

DUNKESWELL ABBEY. Remains of a Perp. gatehouse.

LEIGH (c. Buckland). A small house, but very attractive. There is a charming 15th-century gateway, refectory and dormitory, but the church is gone. The place is occupied as a farm.

Canons

Seculars

EXETER CATHEDRAL. One of the smaller cathedrals, but one of the most beautiful Dec. interiors in the country. It was originally a Norman building, though the only Norman portions remaining are the two transeptal towers. The 14th-century piers, carved corbels and vault are exceptionally good. The exterior, though lacking in dominating or impressive features, is characterized by a quiet dignity. The unusual position of the towers should be noted, also the fine Dec. west front.

There is a rectangular chapter house, and beyond it a corner of the cloister was rebuilt by Pearson to serve as the library.

The various styles are:

NORMAN	Towers.
EARLY ENGLISH	Wall arcade in chapter house.
DECORATED	Lady chapel.
	Choir and nave.
	West front.
PERPENDICULAR	East window.
	Part of chapter house.
MODERN	Part of cloister (a corner of the east and south walks). (Pearson.)
	Reredos (Gilbert Scott).

Vaulted (Tierceron) throughout. It is a magnificent vault.

Total length	383 feet.
West wall to east window . . .	320 ,,
Length of nave	165 ,,
Height of nave	68 ,,
Width of nave	72 ,,
Across transept	136 ,,
Length of choir	130 ,,
Height of towers.	130 ,,
Area	29,000 sq. feet.

Augustinian

CORNWORTHY PRIORY (Nuns). Ruin. Gateway and part of chapel (Dec. and Perp.).

FRITHELSTOCK PRIORY. Ruin; chiefly the west front, with door and three lancets, and part of the north wall.

PLYMPTON ST. MARY PRIORY. A few remains, chiefly the refectory and undercroft, which are incorporated in the Priory Mill.

Premonstratensian

TORRE ABBEY. The existing mansion includes a 14th-century gate-house, crypt of refectory and guest house. Other remains include the chapter house entrance (Transitional), walls of south transept, north wall of north transept, and south wall of presbytery; mainly E.E. It belongs to the Corporation of Torquay.

Dorset

Monks

Benedictine

ABBOTSBURY. There is an exceptionally fine barn, the dovecot and part of a gatehouse.
  Now a farm.

CERNE ABBEY. Perp. gateway, and scanty remains of guest house and a barn.

CRANBORNE PRIORY (c. Tewkesbury). The nave of the church is still in use. It is mainly E.E. of six bays with two aisles, and has a Norman doorway in the north porch, and a Perp. western tower. An E.E. doorway which led from the aisle to the cloister has recently been exposed.
  The chancel is modern (1875).
  There is nothing apart from the church.

HORTON ABBEY. The abbot's house is now the vicarage, and the abbey kitchen the parish hall.
  There are no other remains.

MILTON ABBEY. The choir, transept and tower are Late Dec., and were built from 1392 to 1417 after a fire. The choir is an unusual design, its bays being alternately open arches and solid walls, with clerestory over. The altar-piece is a lofty, niched screen, though the niches are at present vacant.

The south transept has a fine reticulated window, a hanging pyx and a beautiful modern font.

Some Norman fragments from the earlier church are built into the south wall of the choir. No nave seems to have been erected.

The adjoining mansion contains some portions of the conventual buildings, the refectory being the most important.

The whole property belongs to the Church, and is used as a convalescent and rest home.

It may be wondered how it comes about that this abbey stands in a private park, and not in a town or village, as Benedictine abbeys almost invariably do. As things are to-day, the site is suggestive of Cistercian rather than Benedictine surroundings.

The fact is, however, that there was formerly a small market town, called Milton or Middleton Abbas, which adjoined the abbey precincts. It possessed a market place, at least three inns, and a grammar school. After the Dissolution the abbey church was its parish church, while the monastic buildings were converted into a mansion. Matters remained thus until towards the end of the 18th century, when the first Lord Milton, afterwards Earl of Dorchester, removed the grammar school to Blandford, built a new village a short mile away and pulled down the whole town, taking its site into his beautiful park. He provided the village with a new parish church, so that the abbey church ceased to function as such, though services continued to be held there occasionally. At the same time he rebuilt the house, destroying most of the original buildings, though fortunately retaining the refectory, which is now incorporated in it.

This, to a 20th-century mind, somewhat high-handed procedure has resulted in the achievement of much loveliness, for not only is the setting of the abbey church ideal, but the village also is one of outstanding charm.

So here we have a complete reversal of what happened too often elsewhere—viz., the preservation of the town or village and the partial or even total destruction of the abbey, for here it is the abbey that remains and the town that has vanished.

SHAFTESBURY ABBEY (Nuns).   Foundations only.

SHERBORNE ABBEY (Mitred). Mostly a fine Perp. church, with some Norman and E.E. features. It is a cruciform building, and the nave was converted from the original Norman and cased with Perp. panelled stonework. The piers also are panelled. The tower arches are Norman; the tower itself Perp., as also is the very beautiful choir. The north porch is Norman (rebuilt) and the Lady chapel E.E.—partially restored. The " Bow Chapel ", formerly part of a master's house, has reverted to the church, though its

17th-century domestic front has been preserved; it is now the Children's Corner.

The vaulting is a beautiful combination of lierne and fans.

Most of the domestic buildings have been destroyed, though parts of the west range are incorporated in the Sherborne School premises, notably the abbot's hall.

All these buildings, including the church, are of a particularly attractive stone, from Ham Hill quarries.

Total length	.	.	.	.	240 feet.
West wall to east window	.	.	.	195 „
Breadth across transepts	.	.	.	95 „
Breadth of nave	.	.	.	.	60 „
Length of nave	.	.	.	.	70 „
Length of choir	.	.	.	.	66 „
Height of tower	.	.	.	.	109 „
Area	.	.	.	.	15,930 sq. feet.

Cluniac

HOLME PRIORY. Residence, incorporating portions of the conventual buildings.

Cistercian

BINDON ABBEY. Of the church, only the foundations remain. The sacristy, chapter house, daystair, parlour, refectory and kitchen can be distinguished.

FORD ABBEY. There is nothing left of the church, but some of the claustral buildings have been converted into a fine residence, including the Transitional chapter house, the E.E. dormitory with sub-vault, the refectory and part of the north walk of the cloister. The actual cloister walks have gone, except for the small portion of the north walk between the chapter house and refectory. The latter (16th century) and a tower form the entrance hall. The chapter house is used as a chapel. Parts of an older refectory still exist.

The church was to the south.

TARRANT PRIORY (Nuns). Residence, known as " Tarrant Abbey ", which includes the guest house.

No other remains.

Durham

Monks

Benedictine

DURHAM CATHEDRAL. The grandest of all our Norman churches. Situated on an eminence at a bend of the Wear, its three towers form the dominating feature of the city.

The nave and choir are massive Norman work. Each bay is marked by great compound piers, subdivided into two parts by round columns. The latter are variously ornamented with vertical flutings, spirals, lozenges, zig-zag, etc.

The nave vault is contemporary, and is the only Norman high vault in England. It is interesting to note how the transverse arches, in order to reach the required height, are pointed. This is probably the earliest example of the pointed arch in the country.

The choir vault, though of a similar general character, is later, dating from the E.E. period. The easternmost bay of the choir is pure E.E., as is also the eastern transept beyond it—known as " the Nine Altars ". St. Cuthbert's shrine stood immediately behind the altar screen.

At the west end is a lovely late Norman " Galilee " porch, afterwards used as the Lady chapel. It contains Bede's tomb.

The western towers are Norman below, E.E. above; the central tower is Perp.

The cloisters are poor, the openings having unglazed 18th-century tracery, though the west range consists of a fine dormitory (now the library) and undercroft. The site of the refectory is occupied by a 17th-century building (*c.* 1662), used as a museum.

The chapter house is largely a modern building in Norman style upon the original foundations—a memorial to Bishop Lightfoot.

The various styles are as follows :

NORMAN
  Nave, with vault.
  Choir.
  Great transept.
  Lower parts of western towers.
  Galilee.
  Chapter house doorway.

EARLY ENGLISH   Choir vault.
Eastern bay of choir.
The " Nine Altars ".
Upper stories of western towers.

DECORATED   West window.
Altar screen.

PERPENDICULAR   Cloisters, though the windows are unglazed 18th-century work.
Dormitory.
Central tower.

17TH CENTURY   Museum on site of refectory.

MODERN   Chapter house.

The cathedral is vaulted throughout.

Total length	470 feet.
West wall to east window . . .	410 ,,
Length of nave	205 ,,
Height of nave	72 ,,
Width of nave	81 ,,
Width across transept . . .	165 ,,
Length of choir	133 ,,
Height of central tower . . .	218 ,,
Height of western towers . . .	144 ,,
Area . . . . 44,400 sq. feet.	

FINCHALE PRIORY (c. Durham).   Ruin in charge of the Office of Works.   There are extensive remains of the church and the conventual buildings.   They date from the middle of the 13th century, when the church was aisled, as may be seen from the existing arches, which were walled up in the 14th century.

The priory was mainly used by the Durham monks as a convalescent home.

JARROW PRIORY (c. Durham).   The principal interest of this former Saxon abbey lies in its association with Bede, whose home it was for nearly the whole of his life.   The little chancel and the supporting arches of the central tower are Saxon in the main, and still very much as he knew them.   The east window, however, is a Dec. one of three lights.   The upper part of the tower is Norman, as also are some remains of the cloister buildings on the south and west. The east range is gone.

The nave is modern (Gilbert Scott) and uninspiring.

MONKWEARMOUTH PRIORY (c. Durham).   This establishment was slightly older than Jarrow, and associated with it in Saxon times as a

GUESTHOUSE AND CHAPEL—MALLING ABBEY.

WEST RANGE—DAVINGTON PRIORY.

CENTRAL TOWER—TEWKESBURY ABBEY.

Facing page 37.

joint abbey.   All that remains of it are the west wall of the nave of the present church, and the porch forming the base of the western tower.   The upper part of the tower is early Norman.   The rest of the building is later, almost entirely Victorian, and poor.   No other remains.

NEASHAM NUNNERY.   Residence, called " Neasham Abbey ", which has some relics of the old buildings incorporated in it.

Essex

Monks

Benedictine

BARKING ABBEY (Nuns).   Part of gateway (Perp.).

CASTLE HEDINGHAM (Nuns).   Slight remains incorporated in a farmhouse.

COLCHESTER ABBEY (Mitred).   Only the fine Perp. gatehouse is left.   It is a splendid piece of flushwork.

HATFIELD PEVERIL PRIORY (c. St. Albans).   The present parish church built of flint and brick includes the Norman nave (five bays) and north aisle, Norman chancel arch, Norman west door, and turret, of the priory church.   The chancel, south arcade and south aisle are modern.   Apart from the church there are some slight remains.

HATFIELD REGIS PRIORY (c. Rennes).   The nave of six bays still constitutes the parish church.   It is mainly Perp. (plain), with clerestory and aisles, south porch and western tower.   There is some Norman work.   The eastern arm and crossing were demolished.   Nothing apart from the church.

WALDEN ABBEY.   The stables of Audley End are formed from the guesthouse.   There are no other remains.

Cluniac

PRITTLEWELL PRIORY.   Ruin; refectory good.

STANESGATE PRIORY.   Scanty remains.

Cistercian

COGGLESHALL ABBEY.   Slight remains.

TILTY ABBEY.   Merely a portion of wall.

Canons

Augustinian

BICKNACRE PRIORY.   The chief relic is the crossing (Transitional).

COLCHESTER PRIORY.   Ruined Norman nave of church only, partially of Roman brick.   The west front is good.   (Office of Works.)

LITTLE DUNMOW PRIORY.   The south choir aisle and a portion of the choir adjoining form the parish church; the north wall is modern.   It consists of five bays, Norman and Dec., and was restored in 1872.   There is a modern belfry.   The foundations of the central tower and north transept were excavated in 1913–14. No other remains.

LATTON PRIORY.   Some remains (Dec.) now used as a barn, chiefly the crossing.

ST. OSYTH'S PRIORY.   A residence, including the fine Perp. gatehouse, abbot's house and west range of cloister (E.E.).   There is also some Norman and Dec. work, and the tithe barn still remains. It is a splendid group of buildings.

THOBY PRIORY.   Slight remains only.

THREMHALL PRIORY.   Slight remains only.

WALTHAM ABBEY (Mitred).   Originally a minster.   The present church consists of a fine Norman nave of seven bays built *c.* 1050–60 by the Secular Canons then in possession, though it is sometimes stated to have been built by King Harold.   It is a very massive structure, having compound piers alternating with round columns, the latter ornamented with zigzag and spirals similar to those at Durham.   The triforium as now existing is open to the aisles, and there is a fine Norman clerestory.   The present east wall is built inside the western arch of the now vanished central tower.

The western tower dates from 1556.

The Augustinians came into possession about 1177, and the abbey became a great and powerful establishment.   Very little of their work remains to-day—chiefly the gateway, and the entrance to the former cloisters.

Premonstratensian

BEELEIGH ABBEY.   Residence, incorporating chapter house (E.E.) and other portions.

Gloucester

Monks

Benedictine

BRISTOL: ST. JAMES' PRIORY (c. Tewkesbury). The two arcades of the nave, of five bays (Late Norman with clustered piers), form part of a parish church. The lower part of the west front has been restored, but the upper part, with a beautiful circular window, is original. There is a late tower at the east end of the south aisle. Both aisles are modern, and unsatisfactory. Chancel destroyed.

DAGLINGWORTH PRIORY (Nuns). There is a dovecot and some arches.

DEERHURST PRIORY (c. St. Denis, near Paris). The nave is the parish church. South aisle is 12th century, north aisle later. Arcades E.E. Windows Dec. and Perp. The most interesting feature is the Saxon tower (western).

There are some slight remains and foundations of the sanctuary outside the present east wall; also an interesting Saxon building near by, called Odda's Chapel.

GLOUCESTER CATHEDRAL. Formerly a mitred abbey. This is an imposing cruciform building with a majestic central tower (Perp.). While there are Norman characteristics externally, the general effect is of a Perp. building. The Norman parts are more prominent internally, and comprise most of the nave, also the main structure of the choir under its Perp. casing.

The outstanding features of the Norman nave are the great cylindrical columns, rising to a height of over 30 feet. Above them is a small, though very beautiful, triforium. The vault is E.E., and not very successful. The two western bays of the nave are Perp.

The choir is Norman work cased with an elaborate Perp. " skin " of panelling, leaving the original arcade and triforium visible behind it. The triforium is a large and impressive one; the north and south sides of it are connected round the east window by a " whispering " gallery.

The east window is a huge Perp. affair, the largest in Europe, though opinions vary as to its artistic merit.

The Lady chapel is Late Perp., and the largest in England.

The cloisters are extremely fine, with fan vault (the earliest example). The chapter house opens off its east walk, and is partly Norman, partly Perp. (east end). It is a rectangle.

Of the monastic buildings there remain the library and the prior's house (now the Deanery); one wall of the refectory; an arcade of the infirmary; and the Little Cloister. Also two gatehouses.

The various styles are :

NORMAN   Nave (except western bays).
Walls of choir, north transept, presbytery and western part of chapter house.

EARLY ENGLISH   Vault of nave.

DECORATED   Windows and vault of south aisle.

PERPENDICULAR   South transept.
Casing of choir, presbytery and north transept.
Lady chapel.
Cloisters.
Tower.
West front and two bays of nave.
Eastern part of chapter house.
South porch.
East window, and others.

19TH CENTURY   Reredos (Gilbert Scott).

Total length	407 feet.
West wall to east window . . .	315 ,,
Length of nave	174 ,,
Height of nave	68 ,,
Width of nave	80 ,,
Width across transept . .	135 ,,
Length of choir	140 ,,
Length of Lady chapel . .	90 ,,
Height of tower	225 ,,
Area	30,600 sq. feet.

Vaults : Early English   Nave.

Lierne   Transepts.
Choir.
Lady chapel.

Fan   Cloisters.

One of the chief claims of Gloucester Cathedral on the affections of English people lies in the fact that the Perp. style was born there, and some of its achievements are among the most notable in that style, e.g., the tower and the cloisters. Subsequently it spread all over England, and may be seen in various forms in most cathedrals and abbey churches, and in hundreds of parish churches.

The style is peculiar to England.

STANLEY ST. LEONARD'S PRIORY (c. Gloucester). A small, cruciform, aisleless church with a sturdy central tower, having a prominent stair turret. Considerable Norman work remains in the nave and south transept; the chancel (originally Norman) is partly Dec. and has a three-light Dec. east window.

Some traces of the outer buildings are discernible in a neighbouring farm, also remains of a former Saxon church, now a barn.

TEWKESBURY ABBEY (Mitred). This is one of the most impressive churches in England. Nave, transepts and central tower are Norman, and the eastern limb Dec., though resting on Norman piers and foundations. The west front embodies the grandest Norman recessed arch in this country, filled in by a window with 17th-century Perp. tracery. The tower ranks as our finest Norman tower, and is possibly the best of its period in Europe.

The nave piers are massive cylinders nearly 31 feet in height, similar to those at Gloucester, which support a splendid lierne vault springing direct from the capitals.   The triforium is small.

The eastern arm, or presbytery, is Late Dec., with a wonderful late lierne (star) vault. It closes with an extremely beautiful apse surrounded by an ambulatory with radiating chapels—a very rare occurrence in this country. Between the piers is a fine series of chantries.

There is a small Norman chapel to the east of the south transept and a larger E.E. chapel to the east of the north transept.

The only remains of the monastery are the panelling of the north cloister walk (with a reconstructed bay), which was similar to that at Gloucester; the gatehouse; and a considerable part of the abbot's lodging.

Total length	.	.	.	.	306 feet.
West wall to east window	.	.	.	255	,,
Length of nave	.	.	.	.	158	,,
Length of choir	.	.	.	.	97	,,
Width of nave	.	.	.	.	71½	,,
Width across transept	.	.	.	122	,,
Height of nave	.	.	.	.	59	,,
Height of tower	.	.	.	.	148	,,
Area	.	.	.	.	25,110 sq. feet.

D

Cistercian

FLAXLEY ABBEY. Residence. The abbot's house is incorporated in the mansion, and there are some slight remains in the grounds.

HAYLES ABBEY. Ruin; chiefly the walls, etc., surrounding the cloister. E.E.

KINGSWOOD ABBEY. The only remains are the Perp. gatehouse and some odd fragments now embodied in nearby houses.

Canons

Augustinian

BRISTOL CATHEDRAL. Formerly a mitred abbey. Although one of the smaller cathedrals, Bristol has many uncommon features of considerable beauty and interest. The most noteworthy is the absence of triforium and clerestory, the vaults springing direct from the pier capitals both in choir and nave, making the aisles almost the same height as the central avenue. This is the only example of its kind in England.

The choir is Late Dec., and half the arch mouldings go straight to the floor with no intervening capital. The east window is a very fine one, both as regards design and glass, and is second only to that of Carlisle. The nave is modern (by Street) based upon the design of the choir, though not a slavish copy of it. The pier capitals, for example, are bolder.

There are two Lady chapels; the elder (E.E.) off the north transept, and the later (Dec.) at the east end.

The night stair remains in the south transept.

The chapter house and its vestibule are Late Norman, and rectangular in plan. It is a very beautiful building. The east walk of the cloister still exists, and there is a narrow modern north walk.

The choir school occupies the site of the refectory.

The gateway, though in Norman style, is a 15th-century rebuilding of the original.

There is a serenity about this cathedral which is extremely pleasing, and which is largely attributable to the structural methods mentioned. It is vaulted throughout; lierne in the choir, tierceron in the nave.

The styles are:

NORMAN	Chapter house and vestibule.
	Part of transepts.
EARLY ENGLISH	Part of transepts.
	Elder Lady chapel.

DECORATED	Choir.
	Lady chapel.
	Newton chapel.
PERPENDICULAR	Part of transepts.
	Central tower.
	Gateway (Norman style).
19TH CENTURY	Nave. (Street.)
	West front and towers. (Street.)
	North walk of cloisters. (Street.)
	Reredos. (J. L. Pearson.)

Total length	.	.	.	.	300 feet.
Length of nave	.	.	.	.	125 ,,
Height of nave	.	.	.	.	52 ,,
Width of nave	.	.	.	.	69 ,,
Width across transept		.	.	.	110 ,,
Height of central tower		.	.	.	133 ,,
Area	.	.	.	.	22,500 sq. feet.

CIRENCESTER ABBEY (Mitred).   Transitional gateway only.

GLOUCESTER ST. OSWALD'S PRIORY.   Only one wall standing. There are some features, such as doorway and windows, which are hidden by ivy.

LLANTHONY SECUNDA PRIORY, GLOUCESTER.   Originally a daughter house of Llanthony (Mon.).   The principal remnants are of the gateway and wall, the barn, and parts of the prior's house. The latter form part of a farmhouse.

Gilbertine

POULTON PRIORY.   There are some fragments of the church incorporated in the modern parish church, but they are not " in situ ".

Friars

Franciscan

GLOUCESTER.   The remains are incorporated in a wine and spirit warehouse.

Dominican

BRISTOL.   A school on the site embodies part of the buildings of the Friary.

GLOUCESTER.   The dormitory and refectory are converted into two residences.

Hampshire

Monks

Benedictine

ANDWELL PRIORY. The remains of the chapel form a barn.

HYDE ABBEY. Only a few doubtful remains left, but the tower of St. Bartholomew's Church near by is said to be built from abbey material.

MONK SHERBORNE PRIORY (c. St. Vigor, Cerisy). A small alien house, suppressed by Henry V. The unaisled chancel and low tower of the church now serve as Pamber parish church. It is Norman and E.E. Nave and transepts gone.

ROMSEY ABBEY (Nuns). This is the largest and finest nuns' church remaining. It is a cruciform building with a low tower at the crossing. The choir, transepts, tower and eastern half of the nave present a splendid example of Norman work, with compound piers and a large triforium. The western half of the nave is E.E., including the west front. There are two Dec. east windows, and two more in the eastern ambulatory.

The conventual buildings have been destroyed, though in the walk of the cloister abutting on the nave is a very ancient crucifix, said to be Saxon. The chapter house is reputed to have been hexagonal.

Total length	240 feet.
West wall to east windows . . .	216 „
Length of nave	133 „
Width of nave	72 „
Height of nave	70 „
Width across transept . . .	126 „
Length of choir	56 „
Height of tower	92 „
Area . . . . 21,470 sq. feet.

WINCHESTER CATHEDRAL. The longest cathedral in Europe. The oldest part is the transept, which is Early Norman; and the tower, Late Norman.

The nave is one of the most majestic in England, and was originally Norman with a general resemblance to the transepts. In the late 14th and early 15th centuries it was entirely remodelled in the then new Perp. style, and the work was carried through primarily by

DETACHED BELL TOWER—EVESHAM ABBEY.

PRIORY CHURCH—CARTMEL PRIORY.

Facing page 44.

HIGH ALTAR (MEDIEVAL STYLE)—ROMSEY ABBEY.

Bishop Wykeham, who completely altered the character of this part of the church without actually rebuilding it.   Much of the Norman work is still to be seen behind the existing masonry, and the vaulting shafts are the original Norman ones—large, single shafts, rising without break from floor to vault.   The general design of the nave bears strong resemblance to that of Canterbury.

The presbytery, lying to the east of the tower, has Dec. arcades, though its aisles and vault are Perp.

The altar screen is a magnificent piece of Perp. work, probably the finest altar screen in existence, though that at St. Albans is almost as fine.   The processional path behind the screen is E.E.

The only portions of the monastic buildings still standing are the prior's lodging (now the Deanery) and the fine ruined Norman entrance to the former chapter house, now destroyed together with the cloister and its other buildings.

There are some exceptionally fine chantries in this cathedral.

The principal styles are :

NORMAN	Transepts.
	Crypt.
	Tower.
	Core of nave piers and walls.
EARLY ENGLISH	Retro-choir.
	Eastern chapels.
DECORATED	Presbytery arcades.
PERPENDICULAR	Nave.
	West front.
	Lady chapel.
	East window.
	Reredos and altar screen.

The nave and presbytery are lierne vaulted; the transepts have a wooden ceiling.

Total length	526 feet.
West wall to east window . . .	400 ,,
Length of nave	242 ,,
Length of choir	150 ,,
Height of nave	78 ,,
Width of nave	88 ,,
Width across transept . . .	208 ,,
Height of tower	140 ,,
Area	53,480 sq. feet.

Cistercian

BEAULIEU ABBEY.   The gatehouse is adapted as a residence, and the refectory is used as the parish church.   It is E.E. with lancet windows and a Perp. roof, and retains its reader's pulpit.   The ruined E.E. arches of the chapter house still stand on the east side of the cloister; on the north is a row of lancets and an E.E. doorway leading into the church; on the west side are the lay brothers' quarters.

There are only fragmentary remains of the walls of the church, though the foundations are indicated.   Some portions of the precinct wall still exist, with an E.E. gateway.

NETLEY ABBEY.   A small but beautiful ruin, in the care of the Office of Works.   It includes most of the church, sacristy, chapter house, parlour and door of refectory, together with other slight remains.   Mainly E.E.

It was a daughter house to Beaulieu.

QUARR ABBEY, ISLE OF WIGHT.   Ruin; including precinct wall, portions of west and north ranges of cloister, and parts of refectory and outer buildings.   Chiefly E.E.

WINTNEY PRIORY (Nuns).   An interesting site, surrounded by a diverted stream.   The only pre-Dissolution buildings are some barns.

Canons

Augustinian

CHRISTCHURCH PRIORY.   Originally a minster, becoming Augustinian in 1150.   The existing nave was built by the Secular Canons between 1093 and 1099, and is a fine example of the three-storied Norman of the period, with compound piers of the East Anglian type.

The choir is Tudor, and has a good Jesse reredos (14th century) much mutilated.

The Lady chapel is Perp.

There is a 15th-century western tower, but no central tower.

The transept has some very interesting Norman work externally.

Vaults: Eastern arm lierne;
         Nave modern wooden quadripartite.

Total length	306 feet.
West wall to reredos	218 ,,
Length of nave	118 ,,
Width of transept . . .	101 ,,
Length of choir	70 ,,
Height of choir	63 ,,
Width of choir	58 ,,
Area	18,300 sq. feet.

Apart from some slight remains in the grounds of the " King's Arms " Hotel, there are no traces of the monastic buildings.

MOTTISFONT PRIORY. Now a residence, incorporating portions of the conventual buildings, chiefly a part of the cloister and some cellars.

PORCHESTER PRIORY. A small church, of which the Norman unaisled nave and north transept are still in use. Originally the chancel roof was as high as that of the nave and transept, but the present chancel is small. There is a low tower at the crossing, just high enough to receive the roofs. The Norman west front, though small, is good. The south transept is destroyed. No other remains.

The priory was removed to Southwick (*q.v.*) before the close of the 12th century.

PORTSMOUTH CATHEDRAL. The present presbytery, with short transepts (Trans.), originally formed the choir of the priory church of St. Thomas-à-Becket. The rest of the building as it now exists dates partly from 1691, and partly from the present day. Considerable extensions westward are in course of construction.

SELBORNE PRIORY. Foundations and lower courses of the walls of the church.

SOUTHAMPTON PRIORY. The remains of this priory have been rebuilt in the grounds of the County Historical and Antiquarian Museum, having been removed from their original site in Priory Avenue, St. Denys's.

SOUTHWICK PRIORY. Undercroft of refectory only. The priory of Porchester was transferred here, probably in the 12th century, though most of the church still exists at the earlier site, and very little of anything at the later one.

Premonstratensian

TITCHFIELD ABBEY. Ruin. It was adapted after the Dissolution as a residence, now itself a ruin. Part of the nave and cloister remains, and a good deal of the chapter house entrance. E.E.

Hereford

Monks

Benedictine

CRASWALL PRIORY. Scanty remains, including lower courses of east end of the church, and the chapter house. Now a farm. It was a Grandmontine house.

LEOMINSTER PRIORY (c. Reading). Part of the church remains in use as the parish church, and consists of the original Norman nave with a north aisle, and a large Dec. and Perp. second nave with aisle to the south of it, considerably restored. There is a north-west tower, the lower part of which is Norman, upper stage Perp.

The Norman nave was part of the priory church, the Dec. and Perp. portion having always been parochial.

The choir, transepts and monastic buildings were destroyed.

Cistercian

DORE ABBEY. In Charles I's reign, John 1st Viscount Scudamore restored the choir and transepts, and built a tower in the angle between the south transept and the choir from material lying to hand.

The choir is of three bays, and there is an ambulatory behind the altar. All E.E. It is a beautiful fragment.

There is nothing else above ground but a few portions of wall.

The chapter house, of which the foundations alone remain, was twelve-sided.

Length from west wall to reredos .	.	84 feet.
Length from west wall to east wall	.	109 ,,
Breadth of choir and aisles .	. .	63 ,,
Area .	. . .	8,000 sq. feet.

Canons

Secular

HEREFORD CATHEDRAL. One of the lesser cathedrals, mainly Norman in character, though possessing some good E.E. and Dec. work.

The west front is a modern essay in the Dec. style, which harmonises well with the massive Dec. central tower.

The nave arcades are Norman, with round piers and carved

capitals, the easternmost of which are very beautiful, as also are the orders of the arches.   Against each pier are twin shafts, originally the lower portions of the vaulting shafts, but now cut off at the capitals.   The triforium and clerestory on either side date from the 18th century, having been designed by Wyatt after the disastrous fall of the western tower, which was not replaced.

The Norman choir of three bays is a fine example, and there is a splendid Norman arch behind the High Altar.

The south transept is mainly Norman, the north is Geometric of a sharply pointed character.   The Lady chapel is a beautiful E.E. building with a crypt.

The chapter house was a decagon, only the lower courses of which remain.

The cathedral is vaulted throughout.

The distribution of styles is :

NORMAN   Nave arcades.
                 Arcade and triforium of choir.
                 South transept.
                 Retro-choir.

EARLY ENGLISH   Lady chapel and crypt.
                 Choir clerestory.

GEOMETRIC   North transept.

DECORATED   Choir transepts.
                 Aisle walls and windows.
                 Central tower.

PERPENDICULAR   Cloisters.
                 North porch.
                 Windows in south transept.

18TH CENTURY   Nave triforium and clerestory.

20TH CENTURY   West front.

MEASUREMENTS

Total length	326 feet.
West wall to east window . . .	230 ,,
Length of nave	135 ,,
Height of nave	64 ,,
Width of nave	73 ,,
Length of choir	75 ,,
Height of tower	165 ,,
Width across transepts . . .	144 ,,
Area	26,320 sq. feet.

Augustinian

ACONBURY PRIORY (Nuns).   The chapel still exists.   It is an aisle-less building without a chancel, and has a small spire.   A farm occupies the site.

FLANESFORD PRIORY.   Now a farm.   The barn is the principal relic.

WIGMORE PRIORY.   Also a farm.   The house includes part of the prior's lodging.   There is a gateway, of which the upper part is half-timbered; also fragments of the church.

Friars

Dominican

HEREFORD.   There are appreciable remains of this friary, including a wall of the refectory, and a preaching cross.

Hertfordshire

Monks

Benedictine

ST. ALBANS CATHEDRAL.   Formerly a mitred abbey.   This is a very large building, its nave being the longest in England, and its total length second only to that of Winchester.

The nave is partly Norman, built of Roman brick; partly E.E. and Dec. built in stone.   The transepts and central tower are also Norman and built of Roman brick.

The altar screen is a splendid piece of Perp. work, closely resembling that of Winchester.

At the tenth bay stands the rood screen—the only one left in its normal surroundings.   Others remain at Dunstable, Bolton, Davington, Binham and Wymondham, where they form the base of the present east wall of those churches; and at Boxgrove, where it forms the base of the present west wall.

The principal styles are:

SAXON	Baluster shafts in transept triforium.
NORMAN	Nine bays of north nave arcade.
	Three bays of south nave arcade.
	Three bays of presbytery (walls).
	Transepts.
	Central tower.

EARLY ENGLISH	West end of nave.
	Presbytery.
	Saint's chapel.
DECORATED	Five bays of nave (south).
	Lady chapel.
MODERN	West front.
	Five Sisters Window.
	Rose Window.

The presbytery is vaulted in wood; the nave and transepts have wooden ceilings.

Nothing is left of the cloisters, chapter house or other monastic buildings, apart from the gatehouse, which is now the Grammar School. This is a Perp. building.

Total length	520 feet.
West wall to east window . . .	415 ,,
Length of nave	276 ,,
Width of nave	75 ,,
Width across transept . . .	175 ,,
Height of tower	144 ,,
Area	40,000 sq. feet.

CHESHUNT PRIORY (Nuns). Vestiges only.

Friars

Franciscan

WARE. Residence, incorporating part of the cloister.

Huntingdon

Monks

Benedictine

RAMSEY ABBEY. The only remains are part of a Perp. gateway and some E.E. arches of the refectory. The latter are embodied in Lord de Ramsey's seat.

The tower of the parish church, built after the Dissolution, is said to be of material from the abbey. It dates from the 17th century.

ST. IVES PRIORY.   A few walls only, in a private garden.   They have no special feature.

Cistercian

SAWTRY ABBEY.   Site only, marked by mounds.

Kent

Monks

Benedictine

ST. AUGUSTINE'S ABBEY, CANTERBURY. This ancient Religious House was founded by St. Augustine in 598, in the same year as the cathedral, and was the earliest Benedictine abbey to be established in England. Its dedication was originally to SS. Peter and Paul, the name of its founder probably being added by St. Dunstan in 978. It was the home of St. Augustine and his companions, for the cathedral—adapted from King Ethelbert's palace, which he placed at the Saint's disposal—was his metropolitan church *simpliciter* with no monastery attached. Subsequently it became the place of burial of St. Augustine and his five immediate successors, also of King Ethelbert and Queen Bertha.

The oldest of the existing remains are the lower courses of the walls of the church of St. Pancras, built and dedicated by St. Augustine. This building was of Roman tiles or bricks set in a hard mortar, and had a chapel on both north and south sides of the nave, an apsidal sanctuary, and a narthex at the west end. The Saxon apse was taken down in the 14th century and replaced by a square-ended termination.

The abbey church itself lies to the west of St. Pancras. The original floor and foundations of Augustine's church have been excavated; they lie beneath the Norman church which was afterwards built on the site, and show the plan to have been similar to that of St. Pancras. In the chapel on the north side of the nave were the graves of St. Augustine and the five succeeding archbishops—SS. Laurence, Mellitus, Justus, Honorius and Deusdedit. St. Augustine's resting-place was on the south side of the altar of St. Gregory, St. Laurence's on the north, while the graves of Deusdedit and Justus occupied the corresponding corners at the west end of the chapel, with that of Mellitus between Laurence and Justus. The available space being then fully occupied, the three

STALLS—WINCHESTER CATHEDRAL.

PULPITUM—CANTERBURY CATHEDRAL.

Facing page 53.

following archbishops, Theodore, Berchtwald and Tatwine, were buried in the nave, though in 740 Nothelm was interred beneath the chapel altar.

On the south side of the nave, in St. Martin's Chapel, were the graves of Ethelbert and Bertha and of her chaplain, Bishop Lethard.

About 618, King Eadbald, son of Ethelbert, built the Chapel of of St. Mary to the east of the abbey church, and was himself buried there, as were other Saxon kings.

At a later date, possibly in the second half of the 8th century, the abbey church was extended westward and a western tower added. The best authorities are of the opinion that the name of St. Augustine was added to those of the two Apostles when this extension was dedicated by St. Dunstan in 978.

About the middle of the 11th century the abbey church was linked up with St. Mary's Chapel by the erection of an octagonal tower, which involved the demolition of the apse of the church and the west wall of the chapel.

The remains of all these buildings are little more than foundations, for shortly after the Conquest they were pulled down to make way for an imposing new church, to which—in 1091—the bodies of St. Augustine and the other archbishops were removed. The bodies of Ethelbert and Bertha were also re-interred in the new church, and an eye-witness account of these events is still extant. Excavations have revealed the position of the graves of St. Augustine and the other prelates, also those of some of the Saxon kings, though the later graves of Ethelbert and Bertha have not yet been discovered.

The remains of the Norman abbey church are the footings of the west front (underneath later Perp. work), the foundations and lower courses of some of the walls, the north wall of the nave, the two crypts, the north chapel with the graves of three arch-bishops, and some relics of the cloister and dormitory.

The Great Gate of the abbey was built c. 1300, and is in the Dec. style; the Cemetery Gate is some seventy years later. The last addi-tion to the fabric was the 16th-century Lady chapel at the east end.

After the Dissolution the buildings were partially demolished, and partly converted into a royal residence. This residence sub-sequently passed through many hands, being finally abandoned as such early in the 19th century, when it reached its lowest ebb by conversion into a brewery. It was rescued from this ignominy by Mr. Beresford Hope, who in 1843 bought the entire ruins and precincts, carried out a scheme of restoration, and—with the Rev. Edward Coleridge of Eton—founded St. Augustine's Missionary College, the architect being Butterfield.

The existing college buildings include the Great Gateway, the Cemetery Gate, the guest hall, the outer chapel (enlarged) with its crypt (also fitted up as a chapel), and the crypt of the library.

CANTERBURY CATHEDRAL. The See of Canterbury was founded in 598 by St. Augustine, who received from King Ethelbert his palace to the north of the city and adapted it to the purposes of his cathedral church. It probably consisted in the main of a hall with a raised dais at one end, and rooms leading off it. This building had a chequered history, suffering from many Danish raids culminating in its desolation by fire in 1011 during the prelacy of St. Alphege, whom they shortly afterwards murdered at Greenwich. In 1022 the Danes, as an act of expiation, removed the body of the sainted archbishop to Canterbury with great pomp and ceremony, and completed the renovation of the cathedral, which had been roofed over in the interval.

Shortly after the Conquest (in 1067) the cathedral was again destroyed by fire, and a complete rebuilding in the new Norman style was effected by Archbishop Lanfranc, and consecrated in 1077. Lanfranc's successor, St. Anselm, appointed Ernulph as prior, and he seems to have been dissatisfied with Lanfranc's church, demolishing the choir and rebuilding it on a more lavish scale. He died before the work was finished, and his successor, Prior Conrad, carried the plan to its completion, the dedication taking place in 1130.

In 1174 this "glorious Quire of Conrad" was almost totally destroyed by fire, and its rebuilding was entrusted to William of Sens, who, after carrying his work as far forward as the chapels of St. Andrew and St. Anselm (part of Conrad's choir), had the misfortune to fall from a scaffolding in 1178 and be rendered helpless. The completion of the work was undertaken by William the Englishman, who was responsible for the Holy Trinity Chapel and the curious eastern adjunct known as Becket's Crown, or the Corona. Early in the 14th century much beautiful carved screenwork was added by Prior Eastry.

Meanwhile Lanfranc's nave was still in being, but in 1376 and the following years the old nave was pulled down with the exception of the north-west tower, and the present magnificent Early Perp. nave erected on the same foundations under Prior Chillenden, who also finished the reconstruction of the cloisters and chapter house. With the building of the two chapels to the east of the Great Transept and the rebuilding of the south-west tower in the middle of the 15th century, together with the completion by Prior Goldstone of the glorious central tower at the end of the century, the cathedral finally took the form we know to-day, except that the north-west tower of Lanfranc's nave was pulled down in 1832 and the present one erected. This unfortunate decision was made in order to balance the design of the west front.

On entering the precincts through the 16th-century Christ Church Gate one is immediately under the spell of this superb building, the proportions of which—notwithstanding the various dates of its different parts—leave nothing to be desired. The great central tower—known alternatively as the Angel Steeple or Bell Harry Tower—dominates the entire design. Westward from it all is Perp. (chiefly Chillenden's work); to the east Norman (Ernulph and Conrad) and Transitional (the two Williams).

The nave is entered through the south-west porch, when its grace and loftiness are at once apparent. Here, to a greater extent than anywhere else in this country, everything is subordinated to the vertical line, the great clustered piers rising unbroken from floor to vault, while the lateral arches are in one order only, thus leading the eye upward. Note also the beautiful "strainers" across the tower arches to strengthen them against the thrust of the central tower.

The Great Transept is also in the main the work of Chillenden, though the lower parts of the walls of the northern arm belong to Lanfranc's church. This was the scene of the martyrdom of St. Thomas, though the Perp. alterations have naturally changed its appearance considerably from the Norman setting of that tragic event. The older parts of the walls can be detected by the wide jointing characteristic of early Norman construction.

The choir is separated from the nave by a screen, or pulpitum, the west face of which, bearing statues of the Kings of England, is a Perp. frontal to the original Dec. screen of Prior Eastry, whose work in the choir has already been mentioned.

Apart from its own intrinsic beauty, the choir is the most interesting building of its period in the country, and has been aptly described as "the grave of Romanesque and the cradle of Gothic". Here we see Norman forms, such as round arches and chevrons, making their last appearance, while pointed arches, Purbeck shafts, dog-tooth and other E.E. characteristics herald the revolution in architecture of the following century. The carved capitals of French type, and the well-developed triforium, should be remarked. All this part of the cathedral is the work of William of Sens as far as the twin chapels of St. Andrew and St. Anselm, which are survivals of Conrad's choir. Beyond this point the work assumes a different character, and is that of William the Englishman. This section comprises the Holy Trinity Chapel and the Corona. The piers in the chapel consist of twin columns supporting round arches to north and south, and pointed arches in the apse. The capitals are of similar French type to those in the choir. This extremely beautiful chapel, raised high on a lofty crypt, was the setting of the shrine of St. Thomas-à-Becket. The early 13th-century marble floor shows plain evidences of the enormous traffic of pilgrims to this sacred place, reputed to have been the most magnificent shrine in all Christendom, but of which no vestige is left. Other features to be noted are the famous 12th-century glass, the 15th-century wall-paintings in the choir aisles, the tomb of the Black Prince on the south side of the chapel, and those of various archbishops.

The crypt is entered from the north transept through a fine Norman doorway. It is the largest Norman crypt in England, and owing to being mostly above ground is well lit. Its west wall contains fragments of Roman tiles, and may be the sole relic of St. Augustine's cathedral; at any rate, there is no doubt of its Saxon origin. Most of the crypt is Prior Ernulph's work c. 1100, and was the Lady chapel. Alterations to the piers were effected in the 15th century, and the screens added. Much curious carving is to be seen on the capitals. In the Chapel of St. Gabriel, off the south aisle and below that of St. Anselm in the choir, is a remarkable series of early 12th-century wall-paintings, covering both walls and vault. The Chantry of the Black Prince, beneath the south-east transept, is a re-modelling in Perp. style of the older Norman structure. Queen Elizabeth gave it to the Huguenot refugees for use as their church, and it continues to be so used by their descendants. The eastward extension of the crypt below Holy Trinity Chapel is appreciably loftier, and shows an unexpected architectural advance, being of almost pure E.E. style.

The cloister is entered from the Martyrdom Transept, and, though mainly Perp., has some very good E.E. work, and even some of Lanfranc's. The chapter house is off the east walk, and is a large rectangular room of considerable beauty, the Dec. lower part being Eastry's and the Perp. upper part and windows Chillenden's. The Norman doorway which led to the dormitory is another feature of this walk. Off the north walk are the remnants of the refectory, which, together with the remains of the dormitory and rere-dorter, are the early Norman of Lanfranc.

Other features of great interest and beauty lying outside the church and cloister are the Lavatory Tower and the Treasury, both to the north of the choir, and both Norman; the arcade of the infirmary; and a fragment of the infirmary cloister which may be Lanfranc's work. Farther to the north, and lying east of the Great Dormitory, are the remains of the second and third dormitories, between which and the infirmary is the " Dark Entry ", at whose northern end is Prior Selling's Gate leading into the Green Court.

Round the Green Court were grouped the prior's lodging, the granary, bakehouse, brewhouse, almonry and archbishop's palace. These are very much altered, but by far the most interesting of them is the King's School—formerly the almonry—which retains the 12th-century " Green Court Gate ", the vaults of the Pilgrim's Hall, and above all the lovely and often-pictured Norman staircase and porch, surely the most exquisite piece of Norman architecture to be found anywhere.

The Deanery occupies the eastern side of the Green Court, and slightly to the south of the garden and due east of the cathedral is the Queeningate, through which Queen Bertha traditionally passed to her daily devotions at St. Martin's Church.

The styles of the principal parts of the Cathedral are:

NORMAN	Crypt.
	Lower part of north transept walls.
	Chapels of St. Andrew and St. Anselm.
TRANSITIONAL	Choir.
	Holy Trinity Chapel.
	Corona.
EARLY ENGLISH	Arcading in cloister.
	Doorway from cloister to north transept.
DECORATED	Choir screen.
	Lower part of chapter house.
PERPENDICULAR	Nave.
	Cloisters.
	Most of the chapter house.
	South transept.
	North transept, except lower part of walls.
	Central tower.
	South-west tower.
	Transeptal chapels.
	West face of choir screen.
19TH CENTURY	North-west tower.

Vaults:	Quadripartite and sexpartite	Eastern arm.
	Lierne	Nave and Transepts.

Total length	.	510 feet.
West wall to apse arcade . .	.	450 „
Length of nave	.	185 „
Height of nave	.	80 „
Width of nave	.	71 „
Width across transept . .	.	122 „
Length of choir and apse . .	.	265 „
Height of central tower . .	.	235 „
Height of western towers . .	.	130 „

Area . . . . 43,200 sq. feet.

E

CANTERBURY, ST. SEPULCHRE (Nuns).   Slight remains.

DAVINGTON PRIORY (Nuns).   Part of the church still serves as the parish church.   It is a flint building, and consists of a small square-piered Norman nave with an E.E. north aisle and chapel.   The rood screen forms the base of the present east wall.   The west front is Late Norman, with south-west tower.   The north-west tower is incomplete.   The choir is destroyed, and of the cloister the west range still exists, with some remains of other domestic buildings. All belongs to the Church.   The west cloister buildings are let as a residence.

DOVER: ST. MARTIN'S PRIORY.   There is an Early Dec. gateway, Norman refectory, and guest house; now occupied by Dover College.

LILLECHURCH PRIORY (Nuns).   Portions of walls in a farmhouse.

WEST MALLING ABBEY (Nuns).   Now occupied by an Anglican Sisterhood.

The principal Norman relic is the fine ruined tower.   The cloisters (E.E.) form part of the Community's house, and the south transept (E.E.) has been partially restored for use as their chapel.

The Perp. gatehouse and the chapel (Dec. and Perp.) attached to it have been restored and are again in use.

MINSTER ABBEY, SHEPPEY (Nuns).   The parish church consists of nave and north aisle.   The aisle is 12th century, and was the nuns' chapel, while the nave—mainly E.E.—was the parish church.   The arcade is E.E.   In the aisle are some Saxon windows, and at its west end is the lower portion of an unfinished Perp. tower, with shingled wooden belfry.   The north aisle is really the original building, and not an "aisle" in the accepted sense.   It has a low-pitched roof, whereas the "nave" roof is high-pitched.

The gatehouse also remains, and is a fine example.

MINSTER ABBEY, THANET (Nuns).   This convent ceased to exist in 1011, but there are still some portions of Saxon walls and other remains embodied in the house called "Minster Court", together with some Early Norman work dating from after the Conquest, when the place had become a grange belonging to St. Augustine's Abbey at Canterbury.   The foundations of the nuns' chapel have been uncovered, and show it to have been a small apsidal building.

ROCHESTER CATHEDRAL.   Though one of the lesser cathedrals, there are many interesting features at Rochester, of which the most outstanding is its fine Norman west front, dating from the middle of the 12th century.   Before the 15th-century alterations to it were made and the large Perp. window inserted this must have been one of the most imposing of Norman façades, and even as it now stands it ranks very high, the great portal being particularly impressive.

Most of the nave is Norman, with compound piers pairing latitudinally. The triforium is now open to the aisles, owing to the later raising of the aisle roofs, and the nave ceiling is wooden. The two easternmost bays are Dec.

The choir and sanctuary are very rich E.E., and to realise the original intention of the plan it should be remembered that the High Altar stood at the crossing of the eastern transepts—not against the east wall, as it does at present. A unique feature is the solid walls behind the choir stalls separating choir from aisles, in place of the normal arcades. The choir, which is vaulted throughout, is divided from the nave by a massive 14th-century screen; the niches and statuary in its front are, however, modern.

The present chapter house is a later addition, but is entered through an extremely beautiful Dec. doorway—one of the best things in the cathedral.

The cloisters were destroyed, and the remains are slight; they include fragments of the old chapter house, and the lavatorium with a doorway leading to it. Three gateways also remain.

The principal styles are:

NORMAN	West front (Perp. window).
	Most of the nave.
	Part of the crypt (two west bays).
EARLY ENGLISH	Choir.
	Transepts.
DECORATED	Chapter house doorway.
	Two eastern bays of nave.
	Windows.
PERPENDICULAR	Nave clerestory.
	Lady chapel.
	West window.
MODERN	Tower and spire.
	Chapter house.
	North-west tower.
	Roof of transept.
	Reredos (Gilbert Scott).
	West face of choir screen.

Total length	306 feet.
Length of nave	126 ,,
Length of choir	147 ,,
Width of nave	65 ,,
Width across transept . .	125 ,,
Height of nave	55 ,,
Area	23,300 sq. feet.

Cluniac

FAVERSHAM ABBEY.   Some remains of outer walls.

MONKS HORTON PRIORY.   Residence; incorporating part of a fine Late Norman doorway (the main entrance to the church), a smaller doorway, some Dec. windows and a fireplace.

Cistercian

BOXLEY ABBEY.   The guest house is the principal relic—13th and 14th centuries.

Canons

Augustinian

BILSINGTON PRIORY.   Scanty remains.

CANTERBURY, ST. GREGORY'S PRIORY.   Scanty remains.

LEEDS PRIORY, MAIDSTONE.   Scanty remains; chiefly the gatehouse.

LESNES ABBEY, ERITH.   Scanty remains.

Premonstratensian

LANGDON ABBEY.   Chiefly undercrofts supporting a later house.

ST. RADEGUND'S ABBEY, POULTON.   Portions are used as farm buildings, including the remains of the nave, with a tower on the north side (E.E.).   The refectory has been converted into the farmhouse.   Parts of the chapter house, infirmary and two gates (E.E.) also remain.

Friars

Franciscan

CANTERBURY.   A picturesque portion of this friary stands in a public garden on the banks of the Stour.

Dominican

CANTERBURY.   The Refectory, a 13th-century building, still exists.

Carmelite

AYLESFORD.   The residence called "The Friary" embodies some portions of the original buildings.   This was the earliest Carmelite house in England.

Austin Friars

CANTERBURY.   By the side of the entrance to the Simon Langton Schools from St. George Street is a 14th-century doorway which was part of this friary.

ROOD SCREEN AND PARISH ALTAR—ST. ALBANS CATHEDRAL.

SOUTH TRANSEPT AND NIGHT STAIR—HEXHAM PRIORY.

Lancashire

Monks

Benedictine

LANCASTER PRIORY. This has almost entirely disappeared, only a part of its west wall and south doorway surviving as part of the present parish church. This building was not the church of the priory, though sometimes so called, but was built expressly as a parish church after the extinction of the priory, which was alien. It is chiefly Perp., with some modern additions; the tower is 18th century. There are some magnificent 14th-century stalls in this church, which in all probability came from the nearby abbey of Cockersand. They display a veritable riot of carving.

UPHOLLAND PRIORY. The nave of the present parish church was the choir of the priory church. It is a four-bay Dec. building with two fine arcades, though now shorn of its clerestory. Each pier is composed of four shafts, with moulded capitals. The present chancel is Victorian (1883), and conceived in a Late Dec. style. The priory High Altar stood immediately before the present chancel steps, and probably had a large Dec. window behind it, for at the east end of either aisle there is a Dec. window similar to those in the north and south walls, all of which have very good tracery.

At the base of the east responds, and the eastern faces of the easternmost piers, the masonry suggests that there were formerly wooden screens marking the north and south sides of the sanctuary. To the south there would have been a chapel (probably the Lady chapel), as there is a piscina still extant, while to the north the existence of an aumbry denotes the presence of a sacristy.

The present west wall seems to be of later date, for the windows at that end of both aisles are of poor design. Externally there is a half pier in line with each arcade, but standing free of the tower.

The existing tower is of the normal 15th-century country-church type, with some Dec. features re-worked into it. As the hill rises immediately west of the tower and is of rock, it would not have been possible to build a nave.

There are no marks of a cloister against the south wall, though the most westerly bay is not fenestrated, like the others, but has a small window high up, the space below it being built up. Seen externally, this is obviously later work, and evidently there was formerly a door here which gave access to the domestic buildings.

This is the only Benedictine church remaining in Lancashire.

Cistercian

FURNESS ABBEY. One of the largest and most extensive monastic ruins.   A great part of the church still stands, including the Transitional choir and transepts, and the Perp. western tower.   There is an exceptionally good sedilia (Late Perp.).

The eastern arm is of the orthodox Cistercian pattern, as at Kirkstall and Buildwas.   It has a large Perp. window.

The transepts have a series of chapels on their eastern side.

Of the monastic buildings, the chapter house is a very beautiful E.E. structure, its entrance being one of three round Late Transitional arches similar to those at Fountains Abbey.   Considerable portions also remain of the dormitory undercroft, infirmary and abbot's house.

The site is in the care of the Office of Works.

WHALLEY ABBEY.   This very attractive place is now the property of the Blackburn diocesan authorities, and used for retreats, conferences and other diocesan purposes.   It is consequently a well-cared-for living establishment, and not just a museum piece.

The abbot's house is the best-preserved building, having been in more or less continuous occupation, and the west range is also in a tolerably complete condition.   The walls of the east and south ranges stand to an appreciable height, and include several doorways (Perp.).   It is the intention of the diocesan authorities to restore the east range to its former condition.

The only remains of the church are part of the south wall of the nave and a fragment of the south transept, but the plan of the whole church is exposed, also that of the octagonal chapter house.   The main entrance to the precincts is through a fine Perp. gateway, and there is a smaller one (Dec.) standing across the road outside.

The stalls, or most of them, were removed to the parish church. They have been somewhat restored, but are a fine set.

Canons

Augustinian

BURSCOUGH PRIORY.   Only two piers of the central tower and some foundations remain in a farm.

CARTMEL PRIORY.   This is the only completely intact Augustinian church on the grand cruciform plan with a central tower still remaining in England.   The choir has a Late Norman arcade of two round arches on either side, with a Transitional triforium and Perp. clerestory.   The stalls are 15th-century work with carved misereres, but the canopies are very beautiful early 17th-century work—quite unlike anything else in the country.   The sanctuary is spacious, with a large Perp. east window of nine lights.

The north choir aisle retains its original vault, and has a very good pointed Transitional arch leading into it from the transept. The south choir aisle is the Lady chapel.

The transepts are large, and contain work of all periods from Norman to Tudor. The nave is Perp., but retains a good Transitional doorway, covered by a later porch, on the south side—the principal entrance to the church.

The central tower (Transitional) is of low elevation, but there is a second tower (Perp.) set at right angles upon it, which gives it a very distinctive appearance.

There are no remains of the conventual buildings, which stood upon the north side, apart from the gatehouse.

Total length	.	.	.	.	.	169 feet.
Width across transepts		.	.	.	.	110 ,,
Width of choir with aisles	.		.	.	.	76 ,,
Width of nave	.	.	.	.	.	65 ,,
Width of transepts	.	.	.	.	.	28½ ,,
Area	.	.	.	.	12,920 sq. feet.	

Premonstratensian

COCKERSAND ABBEY. The chapter house is the only remaining building here; its outer walls are modern, but its internal vault and ribs are 13th-century. It is an octagon.

Leicestershire

Monks

Benedictine

LANGLEY PRIORY (Nuns). Scanty.

Canons

Augustinian

BREEDON PRIORY (c. Nostell). The choir of five bays, much altered and restored, and the former central tower (the lower part of which is Norman) comprise the parish church. It is mainly 13th-century, though the present sanctuary was erected in 1927, in E.E. style. Various ancient carved stones (Saxon or Early Norman) are built into the walls, and are perhaps the most interesting feature of the church. It has two aisles, of which the northern is vaulted and private, being the property of Earl Ferrers.

The small south transept serves as the porch and vestry. The north transept and nave have been demolished, but the foundations may be traced.

GRACEDIEU PRIORY (Nuns). Scanty, though fairly extensive remains, chiefly E.E. The church was pulled down.

LAUNDE PRIORY. The residence called Launde Abbey includes one arch of the Norman nave arcade, and a charming Perp. chapel with some contemporary glass which has an E.E. doorway.

LEICESTER, ST. MARY'S ABBEY. Apart from some remnants of the boundary walls, nothing is left of this once wealthy and powerful abbey.

OWSTON PRIORY. A chapel with one aisle and a wide-arched arcade, mainly Dec., which is now the parish church, was attached to the gatehouse. It may have been the priory church proper, or merely the gatehouse chapel. There are no other remains.

ULVERSCROFT PRIORY. The ruins include the Perp. western tower, 14th-century south choir aisle, sedilia and part of the refectory. The prior's lodging is a farmhouse. It was a small establishment, and a cell to Haughmond Abbey, Shropshire.

Lincolnshire

Monks

Benedictine

BARDNEY ABBEY (Mitred). Foundations only.

CROWLAND ABBEY (Mitred). All that is now in use is the north aisle, which was always the parish church. It is Perp., and has a Perp. tower at its west end.

A good deal of the west front of the abbey church is still standing, and is a fine example of E.E. and Dec.

There are also some remains of the crossing (Norman), including a complete rib of one of the tower arches.

DEEPING ST. JAMES' PRIORY (c. Thorney Abbey).

This is a most interesting church, consisting of nave and choir with south aisle, and an unaisled sanctuary. Dividing the nave from the aisle is a very fine Transitional arcade of five bays, with clustered piers. The two most westerly piers have circular caps, the others have square caps to each shaft. The arches are round, with deeply undercut mouldings of E.E. character. The nave arcade extends eastward for two more bays forming the choir, the piers and arches being similar to those of the nave.

Over the five bays of the nave arcade is a beautiful E.E. arcaded and passaged clerestory of thirteen continuous arches, and there are signs that it formerly extended to the two bays of the choir. It had a series of lancets in the 13th century, but in the 14th century the aisle was enlarged and its roof raised, so that the clerestory then ceased to function as such. Five of these lancets are open to the aisle, and four others now walled up may be seen from the aisle.

The aisle itself has a good series of Late Dec. windows, the easternmost bay being different from the rest, having been a chapel. It has two eastern Geometric windows, an E.E. piscina on its north wall, and a Dec. piscina on its south wall. This chapel is now screened off and used as a vestry. At the west end of the aisle is a fine window with unusual tracery, its centre being a Latin cross.

The sanctuary is unaisled, of three bays, with wall arcade on the south side somewhat similar to the nave, though later. There are small Transitional windows in each bay, a fine Transitional sedilia and a double E.E. piscina. The altar stands one bay west of the east wall, the window of which is poor, and quite unworthy of the church.

The lower part of the north wall of the church is Norman, with a built-up Norman arch near the choir, and a smaller one at the west end formerly opening to the cloister, which was on the north. The windows on this side are Perp. insertions.

The western tower and spire were built in 1717.

Of the monastic buildings, only the barn remains.

FREISTON PRIORY (c. Crowland). The nave of nine bays, six Norman and three E.E., still serves as the parish church. The Norman piers are round, with scalloped caps. There is a fine Perp. clerestory, but no triforium. The built-up western arch of the former central tower now closes the church at the east end; it is a splendid pointed Transitional arch, with modern Perp. window (1871) inset. The north aisle is brick (Perp.), and the south rebuilt in 1871 to the original design. Fine Perp. western tower.

There are a few very slight remains of the outer buildings incorporated in the adjoining house.

LINCOLN: ST. MARY MAGDALENE'S PRIORY. Locally known as " Monk's Abbey ". Some remains of the E.E. and Perp. chapel are in a public garden.

SPALDING PRIORY. Some cottages are said to be part of the dormitory. At Wykeham, three miles away, is a ruined Dec. chapel formerly attached to a grange belonging to this priory.

STAMFORD: ST. LEONARD'S PRIORY.   Part of the church is incorporated in a barn.   It has a beautiful 12th-century west front, and a Norman arcade of five bays.   The north wall has disappeared, and the south and east sides are built up with later walls.   A small, but lovely fragment.

Cistercian

HEYNINGS PRIORY (Nuns).   The transept (Late Dec.) was restored in 1630 from the ruins, and serves as Knaith Parish Church.   It is divided into two aisles by a plain brick arcade, the south being intact and the north partly rebuilt.   It was further restored in 1894.
　　Very small church.
　　No other remains.

KIRKSTEAD ABBEY.   Very little left.
　　A chapel (E.E.) formerly attached to the abbey is still in use. It stood outside the abbey gate.

LOUTH PARK ABBEY.   All that remains above ground are fragments of the west front, choir, transept and one nave pier.

REVESBY ABBEY.   Residence.   The existing remains are extremely meagre.

Canons

Secular

LINCOLN MINSTER.   The claim of Lincoln Minster to be our finest and most representative 13th-century church is not likely to be challenged, for here we have the various developments of that century to perfection.
　　The choir, attributed to St. Hugh, is the earliest piece of pure Gothic in the world, having been built at the end of the 12th century, when Norman forms were still in evidence elsewhere. One may instance the contemporary choir of Canterbury in this connection.
　　The nave is early 13th century, of the lancet period, as also is the Great Transept.
　　To the east of St. Hugh's Choir is the " Angel Choir "—one of the most perfect architectural conceptions in existence.   It is in the Geometric style, spacious and well lighted, and in strong contrast to St. Hugh's Choir in that respect.   It takes its name from the series of angels sculptured in the spandrels of the triforium.   It is a wonderful piece of work, and well repays the closest study.   Between the choir and the " Angel Choir " is the Lesser, or Eastern, Transept. St. Hugh's shrine formerly stood in the " Angel Choir ", to house which it was built.

From the crossing of the Great Transept rises the central tower, the loftiest cathedral tower in England, and one of the finest.

The west front retains a considerable portion of the original Norman west front of Remigius, also some later Norman work. A great part of the screen is E.E. The two western towers rise behind this screen, and are perhaps too close together for their height.

The cloisters and chapter house lie to the north of the choir, the north walk of the former being in Tuscan style, having been rebuilt by Wren. The chapter house is a splendid decagon, in lancet style, with a central pier.

The principal styles are :

NORMAN

Central part of west front.
Fragments of first bay of nave.
Parts of west front arcading.
Three lower stories of west towers.

EARLY ENGLISH

Choir.
Nave.
Transepts.
Galilee.
West front screen.
Chapter house and part of cloister.
Lower stage of central tower.
Lower part of altar screen.

GEOMETRIC

Angel Choir.

DECORATED

Upper stories of the three towers.
Chapels.

17TH CENTURY   North walk of cloister.   (Wren.)

18TH CENTURY   Upper part of altar screen.   (Essex.)

Total length	482 feet.
West wall to east window . . .	440 ,,
Length of nave	172 ,,
Height of nave	82 ,,
Width of nave	80 ,,
Width across transept . . .	210 ,,
Length of choir and " Angel Choir " .	225 ,,
Height of central tower . . .	271 ,,
Height of western towers . . .	206 ,,

Area . . . . 44,400 sq. feet.

Sexpartite vaulting throughout the Great Transept ; tierceron in nave and " Angel Choir "; asymmetrical in St. Hugh's Choir.

Augustinian

BOURNE ABBEY.   The nave is still in use as the parish church.   Its arcades are mainly late 12th-century Norman work, with round piers.   The western end of the north arcade is E.E.   The clerestory is Perp., and there is no triforium.   The south aisle is Perp.; the north aisle has been rebuilt.   The chancel also is a reconstruction in rather poor style, though its exterior is built of ancient material. The Perp. east window was formerly at the west end.   The west front is Perp. and E.E., but its triple lancet window is modern, replacing the Perp. window now in the chancel.   West doorway and south-west tower are Perp.; north-west tower is incomplete.

There is a small south transept or chapel (E.E.) and a south porch (Perp.).

SOUTH KYME PRIORY.   The south aisle and an adjoining portion of the nave (Late Dec.) of the priory church now serve as the parish church.   It was considerably altered, added to and rebuilt in 1805. There is a Norman south door.   No other remains.

THORNHOLM PRIORY.   Vestiges only.

THORNTON ABBEY (Mitred).   The chief building still standing is the magnificent Perp. gatehouse.   There are some remains of the south transept, and a beautiful fragment of the Geometric (octagonal) chapter house.   The abbot's lodging is a farmhouse.

TORKSEY PRIORY.   A small church, externally uninteresting, but possessing a good E.E. arcade of three bays.   There is but one aisle (north), a small chancel, and a Perp. western tower (plain).   No other remains, though foundations of a larger church have been traced.   Some doubt exists as to whether or no the present church was actually that of the priory, though the arcade would seem to have formed part of it.

Gilbertine

HAVERHOLME PRIORY.   One pier base.

NEWSTEAD PRIORY.   A vaulted Norman room and a Perp. window in a farmhouse.

SEMPRINGHAM PRIORY.   Nothing but a few mounds marks the site of this famous priory, the home and headquarters of the Gilbertine Order.   It stood not far from the parish church, of which St. Gilbert was rector.   The latter building, much mutilated and restored, is still in use.

STAMFORD COLLEGE.   Part of Gate.

Premonstratensian

BARLINGS ABBEY.   One tower pier, some arcading and other small portions remain, including some Dec. windows in a cottage.

SLYPE—CHESTER CATHEDRAL.

CLOISTER ENTRANCE DOOR—CANTERBURY CATHEDRAL.

Facing page 68.

CLOISTER WALK—GLOUCESTER CATHEDRAL.

LAVATORIUM—GLOUCESTER CATHEDRAL.

RAVENDALE PRIORY.   The small chapel survives.

TUPHOLME ABBEY.   The principal relic is one side of the refectory, with six lancets, and a reader's pulpit with two trefoiled arches.

Friars

Franciscan

LINCOLN.   A portion, probably the dormitory and undercroft, is used as the County Museum.

London

Monks

Benedictine

ST. HELEN'S, BISHOPSGATE (Nuns).   This church consists of two parallel naves, after the manner of the nunnery church at Minster, Sheppey.   The northern one was the nuns' chapel, and their stalls still remain in position.   The southern one was parochial.   The existing church dates from *c.* 1470.   The two naves are separated by a Perp. arcade.

There is no tower, and there are no remains of the convent buildings.

WESTMINSTER ABBEY.   This church has more in common with the great cathedrals in the north of France than with the normal English plan, for it is essentially French, especially the apse, with its ambulatory and chevet of radiating chapels.   The loftiness of the vault and the shortness of the eastern arm are other French characteristics.   There are nevertheless a number of purely English details in every part of the building; for example, the moulded pier capitals, and the bands on the piers.

The finest portions of the church are the apse, transepts and choir, all of which date from the first part of the 13th century.

To the west of the choir screen lies the nave, which is Perp., though harmonious with the choir.   Choir and nave together form the western limb.

The cloisters are very fine, and date from the 13th century. The chapter house is a beautiful octagon with a central pier, partially restored by Gilbert Scott, who also reconstructed the north porch (the main entrance).

Between the High Altar and the apse is the Chapel of St. Edward the Confessor, which contains his shrine.

Henry VII's Chapel, at the extreme east end of the building, is a wonderful piece of Tudor work. It is very elaborate, and has a vault of open stonework which appears to hang in space.

The western front is Perp., and of poor design. Towers are 18th-century (Hawksmoor).

The refectory has gone, but the dormitory belongs to Westminster School, while the Deanery was formerly the abbot's house.

The styles are:

EARLY ENGLISH	Choir.
	Apse.
	Transepts.
	Chapter house.
	Part of cloister.
DECORATED	South and west cloister walks.
PERPENDICULAR	Nave.
TUDOR	Henry VII's Chapel.
18TH CENTURY	Western towers.
19TH CENTURY	North porch (main entrance).
	Altar-piece (Salviati and Gilbert Scott).

Total length	511 feet.
Length of western arm (nave 162 ft.; choir 82 ft.) :	244 ,,
Height	101 ,,
West wall to apse . . .	360 ,,
Width	71 ,,
Width across transept . . .	200 ,,
Height of central tower . .	151 ,,
Height of western towers . .	225 ,,
Area	46,000 sq. feet.

Cluniac

BERMONDSEY ABBEY. Foundations only.

Canons

Augustinian

ST. BARTHOLOMEW'S PRIORY. The existing building consists of choir, transepts, one bay of the nave, the Lady chapel and a restored walk of the cloister.

The choir is a beautiful piece of Norman work, with round piers having cushion capitals, a fine triforium and a Perp. clerestory. The roof is wooden, and there are no vaulting shafts. The apse, which is a modern restoration, carries the design right round, though its bays are only half the width of the north and south arcades, the arches being stilted to reach the same height.

The Lady chapel (Perp.) and the east walk of the cloister have been restored within quite recent times.

This church has suffered many vicissitudes, and has perhaps had a more turbulent history than most others.   Part of the triforium was for a time used as a nonconformist school; the Lady chapel was a fringe factory; the east end was squared off with a hideous wall; the north transept was used as a blacksmith's forge; and the recently restored cloister walk was a stable.

The site of the nave was a burial-ground, and is now a rest garden. Its length is indicated by the continued existence of the western doorway to the former south aisle.   This is a charming E.E. arch-way with a half-timbered first floor added.   It stands on the street, and serves as the entrance to the churchyard.

The devotion of successive rectors since 1863, when the piers of the apse were restored, has enabled these various portions of the church to revert to their proper functions.   A large part of the restoration was done in the nineties, when the upper stage of the apse and the Lady chapel were recovered from secular use and put in order by Sir Aston Webb.

Total length	195 feet.
Length of choir	105 ,,
Width of choir and aisles . . .	54 ,,
Height	47 ,,
Length of Lady chapel . . .	60 ,,
West wall to Lady chapel gate . .	135 ,,
Area	10,000 sq. feet.

SOUTHWARK CATHEDRAL. This beautiful church has passed through almost as many difficulties as St. Bartholomew's.

The choir and transepts are part of the original E.E. building; the restored Lady chapel was for a long time a bakery; and the present nave—the third—is a modern rebuilding, conforming in general style to the choir.   The reredos (restored) is a splendid Perp. screen.

The church is vaulted throughout, the shafts being triple, springing from the pavement and banded at the usual places.

There is a central tower, E.E. in its lower, and Perp. in its upper, stage.

The cloisters, chapter house and monastic buildings are destroyed.

Total length	238 feet.
West wall to east window . . .	202 ,,
Length of nave	106 ,,
Height of nave	55 ,,
Width of nave	60 ,,
Width across transept	115 ,,
Height of tower	130 ,,
Area	17,250 sq. feet.

Friars

AUSTIN FRIARS.   The Perp. nave of the church was a Dutch church up to the recent war, when it was destroyed by enemy action.

Norfolk

Monks

Benedictine

ALDEBY PRIORY.   Portions embodied in farm buildings.

BINHAM PRIORY (c. St. Albans).   The nave of the church continues to serve as the parish church.   It is of seven bays, four Norman and three E.E., with aisles removed and arches walled up.   Windows are inserted in some of them, both in the main arcade and triforium. There is a fine passaged clerestory.   The Norman piers are compound.   The west front is E.E., with a beautiful doorway and a Geometric window (walled up) over it.   The rood screen forms the base of the present east wall.

There are extensive ruins of the choir, transepts, central tower, chapter house, refectory and gatehouse, in charge of the Office of Works.

CARROW PRIORY, NORWICH (Nuns).   The prioress's house (Tudor) forms part of a residence called Carrow Abbey.

There are some remains of the 12th-century church and cloister walls.

HORNING: ST. BENET'S ABBEY (Mitred).   The ruined Perp. gateway is the only feature above ground, though the foundations of the church may be traced.

HORSHAM PRIORY.   Some remains may be seen in a private garden, near the church.

KING'S LYNN (ST. MARGARET'S) PRIORY.   Parts of the church remain in the existing parish church.   The south-west tower is Norman, E.E. and Dec.   The north-west tower is Perp., as also is the west window and door.   The nave and its aisles were destroyed in 1741 by the fall of a spire which formerly surmounted the southwest tower, and it was rebuilt in the depressed Perp. style prevailing in mid-18th century.

The chancel is E.E., with shafted piers carrying foliated capitals; the clerestory is Perp., and has a footwalk. It is a beautiful chancel. The reredos is by Bodley.

The present transepts are much smaller than those formerly existing, being 74 feet in width against 132 feet originally. There is a low lantern tower over the crossing, supported on fine E.E. arches.

The east window is curious, having been originally a wheel; but it has been extended downwards from its full width, and now appears as a round-headed window filled with rectilinear tracery in a circle.

There are two Norman arches supporting the south-west tower, but in the north-west tower the only Norman remnant is an arch out of alignment.

Remains of the monastic buildings are slight and problematic.

Total length of church	235 feet.
Length of choir	80 „
Length of nave	125 „
Width of nave	63 „
Width across transept	74 „
Height of western towers	82 „
Area	14,650 sq. feet.

NORWICH CATHEDRAL. While not rivalling Durham in splendour or majesty, Norwich is one of the best and most complete of our Norman cathedrals. There is Norman work in every bay, even where it does not predominate. There is, too, an unusual lightness and grace about the whole design which gives it a marked individuality. The nave is one of the longest in England, and its triforium is virtually a duplicate of the lower arcade, an unusual feature in a building of this size being the flat soffits to all the arches. The clerestory is late, and the lierne vault magnificent.

The choir and presbytery are very beautiful, the distinguishing feature being the great apse, in which the ground arcade and triforium are of noble Norman compound piers and arches with flat soffits, the two stories being of almost identical size. The clerestory is a lovely Late Dec. structure of considerable height, with a glorious lierne vault. Round the apse runs the original Norman ambulatory—the only one left. There are two Norman chapels radiating from it, north-east and south-east. On the site of the destroyed Lady chapel there now stands the War Memorial Chapel (1914–18).

The tower is Late Norman, but it has been restored, and much of its stonework is new, though retaining its original beauty of design. The spire is Perp.

F

The cloisters (E.E. and Dec.) are among the finest which remain, and possess a wonderful series of bosses.   The chapter house and the other monastic buildings were destroyed.   There is a 13th-century gateway, and a Perp. gateway.

The cathedral is vaulted throughout.

The best view is obtained from the south-east, when the choir, apse, flying buttresses, tower and spire form a most attractive composition.   The view from the west is disappointing, the west front and the exterior of the nave being plain and severe.

The styles are as follows :

NORMAN	Nave.
	Choir triforium.
	Apse.
	Transepts.
	Tower.
EARLY ENGLISH	Entrance to War Memorial Chapel.
	Part of cloisters.
	Ethelbert's Gate.
DECORATED	Part of cloisters.
	Clerestory of presbytery.
	Chapel of St. Mary the Less.
PERPENDICULAR	Ground arcade of presbytery.
	Vault.
	Choir aisle screen.
	Spire.
	Windows.
20TH CENTURY	War Memorial Chapel.

Total length	407 feet.
West wall to apse arcade . . .	387 ,,
Length of nave	212 ,,
Height of nave	72 ,,
Width of nave	72 ,,
Width across transept . . .	178 ,,
Length of choir	165 ,,
Height of choir	83 ,,
Height of spire	315 ,,
Area	34,800 sq. feet.

THETFORD PRIORY (Nuns).   There is an arch (Transitional) belonging to the south transept, and some lesser remains.

WAREHAM PRIORY.   Slight traces of this alien priory may be seen on a farm.

WYMONDHAM ABBEY. The existing church consists of the Norman nave of the abbey church, with Norman triforium, and Perp. clerestory, fine hammerbeam roof, and aisles of nine bays. The rood screen forms the base of the present east wall. There is a large Perp. western tower. This part of the building was always parochial.

It is mostly of flint and stone, and the external appearance is mainly Perp.

At the east end of the church, and outside it, are a late octagonal tower and some slight remains of the monks' choir. A gable end of the chapter house still stands. There are no other remains.

YARMOUTH PRIORY. The only thing left is the 12th-century refectory, now used as a schoolroom.

Cluniac

BROOMHOLM PRIORY. Ruin, comprising portions of north transept (Transitional), chapter house and part of refectory (E.E.), common room (Perp.) and gatehouse (Transitional and Perp.).

CASTLE ACRE PRIORY. Its chief glory is its splendid Norman west front. There are also some remains of the chapter house and some walls of the church. The west range, with the Prior's Lodging (Perp.) and gateway (Perp.), still stands.

THETFORD PRIORY. The fine Perp. gatehouse, and some slight remains near it, are in charge of the Office of Works. The foundations of the church are traceable.

Cistercian

MARHAM PRIORY (Nuns). Some remnants are incorporated in farm buildings.

Canons

Augustinian

BEESTON PRIORY. Ruin, including part of tower, lower portions of walls and the west end of the church (aisleless) E.E.: also foundations of the chapter house.

BUCKENHAM PRIORY. Slight remains.

COKESFORD PRIORY, EAST RUDHAM. Remains of north wall of nave and chancel, with one window.

FLITCHAM PRIORY. Some remains in a farmhouse.

HICKLING PRIORY. Farm. Slight remains.

NORTH CREAKE PRIORY. Ruin; some arches and piers of the choir arcade. E.E.

PENTNEY PRIORY. Gateway.

THETFORD PRIORY. The nave serves as a barn, and the porter's lodge forms part of another outhouse.

WALSINGHAM PRIORY. The remains include a Perp. gateway, part of the east end of the church, a portion of the refectory and other fragmentary ruins. The residence called " Walsingham Abbey " partly incorporates the prior's lodging.

WEST ACRE PRIORY. Some slight remains of the tower of the church, and other portions. The gateway and barn are the chief buildings still standing.

WEYBOURNE PRIORY. Some remnants of the church, principally the tower and an east window, adjoin the parish church in the same manner as at Wymondham, though on a smaller scale.

Premonstratensian

LANGLEY ABBEY. There are some remains of the cloister (Dec.), including a doorway; also an undercroft. Now farm buildings.

WENDLING ABBEY. Part of the west end and some walls of the church may still be seen; also some foundations.

WEST DEREHAM ABBEY. Only a barn, and a few odd fragments.

Friars

Franciscan

KING'S LYNN. The graceful hexagonal central tower still survives, forming the entrance to Tower Gardens, which occupy the site of the friary.

WALSINGHAM. There are some remains on a farm.

YARMOUTH. The remains are the property of the Great Yarmouth Historical Buildings Society.

Dominican

NORWICH. The nave is St. Andrew's Hall—the chief Assembly Hall of the city, and the choir, called Blackfriars Hall, is an annexe to it. It is a good Perp. building, with some late Dec. as well as Perp. windows.

THETFORD. A school occupies the site.

Carmelite

NORWICH. There are some remains.

Austin Friars

THETFORD. There are some remains in the garden of Ford Place.

NIGHT STAIR—TINTERN ABBEY.

DAY STAIR—CLEEVE ABBEY.

Facing page 76.

CHAPTER HOUSE EXTERIOR—HAUGHMOND ABBEY.

CHAPTER HOUSE INTERIOR—VALLE CRUCIS ABBEY.

Facing page 77.

Northants

Monks

Benedictine

CATESBY PRIORY (Nuns). A small modern chapel (1861) contains some old material, including sedilia and piscina; otherwise slight remains only.

PETERBOROUGH CATHEDRAL (Mitred Abbey). The outstanding feature is the magnificent E.E. west front, which has good claims to be regarded as the finest in Europe.

The rest of the cathedral is almost entirely Norman, though at the west end of the nave there is a Transitional transept, and at the extreme east end is a Perp. chapel, or ambulatory, with a beautiful fan vault.

The choir, nave and central transepts are Norman, the choir piers being alternately round and octagonal, the nave piers compound.

The nave still has its original Norman wooden ceiling, while the choir has a Perp. wooden roof.

The east end of the choir is a Norman apse, though the ground arcade has lost a good deal of its Norman character, the openings being square-headed and filled with Dec. tracery. The triforium and clerestory preserve their Norman windows although they also have Dec. tracery. The bays are separated by compound vaulting shafts extending from floor to roof, but there is no vault, the apse having a flat ceiling.

The Lady chapel, chapter house, cloisters and monastic buildings were destroyed, but there are a few remains, notably of the infirmary and the west and south walls of the cloister. There is a western gate (Norman and Dec.) and a Perp. gate.

The central tower is a low one, Perp., rebuilt last century.

The Deanery was formerly the prior's house.

The styles are as follows :

NORMAN   Choir.
                Nave.
                Transepts.

TRANSITIONAL   Western transept.

EARLY ENGLISH   West front.
North-west tower.
Remains of cloister.

DECORATED   West porch.
Various windows.

PERPENDICULAR   " New Building."
Central tower.
North-west spire.
North-east gateway.
West window, and other windows.

Total length	426 feet.
West wall to apse arcade . . .	400 ,,
Length of nave	266 ,,
Length of choir	130 ,,
Height of nave	78 ,,
Width of nave	79 ,,
Width across transept . . .	185 ,,

Area   .   .   .   .   41,090 sq. feet.

Canons

Augustinian

CANONS ASHBY PRIORY.   Stands in private grounds and is privately owned, though the parish has rights.   Only the western portion of the church remains, consisting of two bays with north aisle, in late E.E. style.   The west front is a good composition, mainly late E.E., with a large depressed Perp. window, and is flanked on the north by a Dec. tower erected in 1350.   No other remains.

CHALCOMBE PRIORY.   There are some slight portions of the monastic buildings incorporated in the residence called " Chalcombe Priory ", including remains of the chapel.

FINESHADE PRIORY.   Some slight remains are incorporated in the residence of the same name.

Northumberland

Monks

Benedictine

LINDISFARNE PRIORY (c. Durham). Lindisfarne, or Holy Island, was first settled by monks from the Celtic Church at Iona, and is the cradle of Christianity in the North of England, from which it spread almost throughout the land. St. Aidan and his companions came here in 635, two years after the Danes had virtually extirpated the results of St. Augustine's mission in Kent. Here he set up his monastery after the Celtic fashion, and established the See of Northumbria, of which he was respectively abbot and bishop. Its independence of all outside authority continued until 664, when St. Colman, then the abbot and bishop, with St. Hilda of Whitby, was unable to counter the specious pleadings of St. Wilfrid, who argued at the Council of Whitby in favour of submission to Rome so successfully that the King decided in his favour. St. Colman thereupon returned to Iona, and his successor in the bishopric conformed to the Roman rite. Of his successors, St. Cuthbert is the most celebrated. This establishment was finally and utterly destroyed by the Danes in 875, and remained derelict until it was re-founded by monks from Durham in 1083. It is the remains of this cell of Durham which we now see.

The Office of Works have exposed the foundations and lower courses of the cloister buildings, but the remains of the superb Norman church are the principal attraction. The west front, north wall and transept, part of the north arcade, and the short eastern arm, are still standing; also a flying rib over the crossing. The interior elevation of the west front is very beautiful, as is the splendid arcade (in the Durham style). The church dates from the end of the 11th century, and is the earliest of all our ruined monastic buildings.

TYNEMOUTH PRIORY (c. St. Albans). Considerable remains of the church are left, including a beautiful E.E. presbytery. Part of the rood screen still stands, and a portion of the Norman west front. The sadly mutilated gateway—a military depot—is the only other remnant.

Cistercian

NEWMINSTER ABBEY. Residence. The original work is one doorway and some foundations, but portions of the cloister, chapter house and infirmary have been reconstructed with the original material.

Canons

Augustinian

BRINKBURN PRIORY. The church was a ruin until 1858, when it was restored. It is a cruciform building with a low central tower, a single arcaded nave of six bays with triforium and clerestory, north aisle, and transepts with an aisle on the east side. The chancel is unaisled. The style is mostly E.E., of an unpretentious character, with some Transitional features, and there is a fine Late Norman north doorway. The church is 131 feet in length, and 74 feet across the transept. The south-west corner, and all the gables, are modern restoration.

It is beautifully situated in private grounds on the banks of the Coquet, and is privately owned. There is a residence adjoining.

HEXHAM PRIORY. Formerly there stood on the site of this church a Saxon cathedral founded by St. Wilfrid towards the end of the 7th century. Some extremely interesting portions of this ancient building are incorporated in the present church, the most important being the crypt, approached by a stairway in the nave. This crypt, which has many points in common with Wilfrid's other crypt at Ripon, is built of worked Roman stones, probably taken from the neighbouring Roman city of Corstopitum, some of which bear most interesting inscriptions. Other remains of the Saxon cathedral are the lower courses of part of the west and north walls, which can only be seen outside. They also are of Roman stones. The foundation of the eastern apse may be seen under the floor of the first bay of the chancel. Thus the length of the original minster was about 150 feet.

These very ancient details do not affect the general appearance of the present building, the oldest part of which is the chancel, and dates from the end of the 12th century. It is of late Transitional character, merging into E.E., and has a well-proportioned triforium and clerestory surmounting the beautiful ground arcade, the piers of which are clustered and the arches pointed and well moulded. The present easternmost bay, together with the east wall, is modern work. Formerly there was a 14th-century range of chapels here, and the east window was a large Perp. one, but apparently all this section became dilapidated, and was demolished in 1858, when the present eastern bay was substituted.

The south transept (E.E.) was the next part to be built. It has chamfered arches, but its outstanding feature is the night stair, incomparably the finest one left. There is another at Bristol Cathedral, but it is beyond the south wall, and not in the transept itself. Remains of others are at Tintern and Fountains, but nowhere else is there so splendid an example as Hexham. It leads to a platform over the slype, which occupies the southern bay of the transept floor.

The north transept is somewhat later in style, though still E.E., and is of a more beautiful design than the south. The piers are more graceful, and the arches moulded. The walls are arcaded, and, in short, the design is altogether more fully developed. There are some extremely tall, stilted lancets in this transept, which seem to have been an afterthought, the original intention evidently having been for three tiers.

The nave, with the exception of the lower courses already mentioned, and its eastern bay, is a modern work, having been built as recently as 1908 in 14th-century style. For a long time—ever since 1296—there had been no nave at all. In that year the then nave was destroyed by Scottish raiders, and it is said to have been the original nave of Wilfrid's church.

A unique feature is the wooden pulpitum, a structure invariably of stone in other monastic churches. Attention should also be drawn to the stalls, thirty-six in number, complete with misericordes, though the canopies have vanished.

The external appearance of the church is somewhat mixed, the new work looking very new, and the old stonework—including the E.E. central tower—extremely dilapidated and weather-worn.

The monastic buildings were on the south side, and there are appreciable remains of them. The chapter house has vanished— the street runs over its site—but its E.E. vestibule is tolerably intact. Beyond this are scanty remains of the warming-room, and, on the south side, of the refectory. On the west range are some buildings occupied by the Police, though little of them is noteworthy except the beautiful Geometric tracery of the lavatory— one of the gems of the priory.

Total length	221 feet.
Length of nave	100 ,,
Length of choir	95 ,,
Width of choir	57 ,,
Width of transept . . .	153 ,,
Area	15,900 sq. feet.

Premonstratensian

ALNWICK ABBEY. Gate tower only.

BLANCHLAND ABBEY. The whole village of Blanchland seems to be built of abbey material, and much of it is still where it originally stood. The gatehouse opens into the village square, and the "Lord Crewe Arms" contains parts of the abbot's house. The refectory, store-houses and other outer buildings have been turned into cottages, and while their original form is not apparent without study, there are many surprising features in them.

The existing church is the north transept and chancel of the abbey church, the south transept and nave having disappeared. It is small, and not specially noteworthy, though very interesting from the fact that it is the only Premonstratensian church still in use. An unusual feature is the position of the tower—at the north end of the transept.

Friars

Dominican

BAMBURGH. A ruined wall is all that remains.

NEWCASTLE. The church has gone, but the other three ranges still exist, though mutilated. The chapter house entrance, parlour, part of the refectory and of the west range may be discerned, but the whole place is squalid.

Carmelite

HULNE FRIARY. Occupies a beautiful position on a rise beside the River Aln in Hulne Park (Alnwick Castle). Its remote situation is the explanation of the continued existence of so much of it, for it is by far the most complete of all friary remains.

It is encircled by a wall, but the present entrance is relatively modern, for the place has suffered considerable mutilation and adaptation to other purposes. The church, however, is easily discoverable, and is an unpretentious narrow structure without aisles, the best features of which are at the west end. The "monastic" buildings are difficult to follow, as the plan does not conform to the accepted type, but the sacristy and chapter house are clear enough amid much that is speculative and still more that is post-Dissolution work. Very little remains of the refectory or the west range, and parts of them seem to be relics of some Elizabethan work.

One of the principal items of interest is the Perp. tower erected in 1488—a strong place of refuge in case of Scottish raids.

A thoughtful Duke has enlivened the precincts with some stone figures of friars, doubtless with the idea of "lending an air of artistic verisimilitude". They are friendly fellows, and give the visitor a not unpleasant welcome.

Nottingham

Monks

Benedictine

BLYTH PRIORY (c. Holy Trinity, Rouen).   The early Norman nave
of the church still stands.   It has compound piers, triforium (now
used as clerestory) and north aisle.   The south aisle is a large Dec.
addition, and was originally built to serve as the parish church.
There is a Perp. western tower.

The Norman nave has an E.E. vault.   Nothing remains of the
eastern arm or crossing, and only vestiges of the monastic buildings.

Cluniac

LENTON PRIORY.   Very slight remains.   There is a chapel of ease
to the parish church which is locally known as the " Priory Church ",
but actually it dates chiefly from 1884, though it contains in its
chancel some part of the walls of a former gate chapel, or possibly
hospital chapel.   Nothing is left of the priory church itself, and of
the monastic buildings there are some walls preserved in later
buildings, and two pier bases.

Carthusian

BEAUVALE PRIORY.   The remains are somewhat scanty, and are in
the grounds of a residence called " Beauvale Abbey ".   Excavations
have revealed the prior's house, west end of church, part of the gatehouse, and a few other fragments.

Cistercian

RUFFORD ABBEY.   Residence.   There are some slight remains,
chiefly the refectory, incorporated in the house.

Canons

Secular

SOUTHWELL MINSTER.   This fine minster possesses a Norman nave
in three stories, the piers being circular, and the triforium almost as
massive an arcade as the main series.   The clerestory windows are
circular, and the roof wooden (barrel).

The transepts, west front, western and central towers are all
Norman.

The choir is a beautiful vaulted E.E. example in two stories consisting of the main arcade and a clerestory, with a passage below the latter.

The chapter house is an octagon without a central column, in the Dec. style. The entrance is a particularly beautiful one, usually considered the best of its kind. This chapter house altogether is an exceptionally beautiful building.

The styles are :

NORMAN   Nave.
                Transepts.
                Towers.
EARLY ENGLISH   Choir and chapels.
DECORATED   Chapter house.
                Screen.
PERPENDICULAR   West window, and other windows.

Total length   .   .   .   .   . 300 feet.
Length of nave .   .   .   .   . 150 „
Length of choir .   .   .   .   . 128 „
Width of nave   60   „
Width across transept   .   .   . 121 „
Height of central tower .   .   . 105 „
Height of western spires .   .   . 150 „
Area .   .   .   . 20,480 sq. feet.

Augustinian

FELLEY PRIORY. Residence called "Felley Abbey" incorporates such remains as there are.

NEWSTEAD PRIORY. Usually known as Newstead Abbey. Of the priory church only the fine Geometric west front remains, though the adjoining residence (which was until 1818 the seat of the Byron family) incorporates the prior's lodging, refectory, chapter house and cloister garth. Much of this is considerably altered, and its interest is Byronic rather than Augustinian.

The ruins, house and gardens, together with the gatehouse, are now the property of the Nottingham Corporation, and comprise some 20 acres.

THURGARTON PRIORY. The existing church consists of an E.E. nave of three bays with neither triforium nor clerestory, a north-west tower E.E. in its lower stages, and a modern north aisle and chancel (1853). The west front (E.E.) is good, with a beautiful western doorway.

Apart from a few fragments by the church and the 13th-century undercroft of the adjoining house, there are no remains of the monastic buildings. The west front is in the grounds of the residence, called "Thurgarton Priory".

CHAPTER HOUSE (POLYGONAL) LINCOLN MINSTER.

CHAPTER HOUSE (POLYGONAL) SOUTHWELL MINSTER.

Facing page 84.

PARLOUR—CHESTER CATHEDRAL.

WORKSOP PRIORY. A very fine Late Transitional nave in three stories, with piers alternately round and octagonal. The arches are all round, and the ornament upon them and the capitals is mostly nail-head. There is one real Norman pier at the east end. The Canons' parlour is used as the vestry.

The west front is a severe Norman design, and has two towers, one of which is Norman and the other later.

The central tower, transepts, choir, Lady chapel and monastic buildings were destroyed, but of recent years the south transept has been rebuilt and the Lady chapel (E.E.) restored as a War Memorial (1914–18), and still more recently the north transept and crossing have been rebuilt, using some original material.

The gatehouse (E.E. and Perp.) still remains, and is a fine example.

Length of nave	140 feet.
Width	60 „

Gilbertine

MATTERSEY PRIORY. Mostly lower wall courses, showing the ground plan. In charge of the Office of Works.

Oxford

Monks

Benedictine

COGGES PRIORY. Some slight remains form part of the vicarage.

EYNSHAM ABBEY. Site only.

GODSTOW PRIORY (Nuns). Slight remains only, principally of the chapel (Perp.) and some boundary walls.

MINCHERY PRIORY (Nuns). Some Perp. windows in a farmhouse are the only remnants.

STUDLEY PRIORY (Nuns). Residence incorporating as its north wing the priory chapel, as reconstructed in the 17th century.

Cistercian

REWLEY ABBEY, OXFORD. Portion of east wall, with a Perp. gateway.

THAME ABBEY. Residence, incorporating some very late work, *c.* 1530.

Canons

Augustinian

BICESTER PRIORY.   Part of the guest house is incorporated in " The Old Priory House ".   No other remains.

DORCHESTER ABBEY.   Before the Conquest, Dorchester was the seat of a bishopric which extended from the Thames to the Humber, but in 1092 the See was transferred to Lincoln and the importance of Dorchester declined.   In 1140 Bishop Alexander of Lincoln remedied this to some extent by establishing here an Augustinian abbey.

There are no remains of the Saxon cathedral, and it is not unlikely that the existing Augustinian church occupies its site.   This is a beautiful church, mainly Dec., though retaining its Norman north nave wall and Transitional chancel arch.   Its structure is unusual, having a nave with a large south aisle, and a spacious chancel with two aisles, the south aisle containing two chapels.   The east window and the north sanctuary window are remarkable for their unusual designs.   There are no long lights, but the tracery of the east window extends from the base to the top, and in the north window it is of irregular design forming the branches of the Tree of Jesse.

The part of the building east of the chancel arch was the conventual church, while the nave and aisle were parochial.

There is an early 17th-century western tower, and of the monastic buildings only one (said to be the guest house) was preserved for use as a Grammar School.

Total length	.	.	.	.	192 feet.
Breadth of nave and aisle		.	.	.	53 ,,
Breadth of chancel and chapels		.	.	70 ,,
Area	.	.	.	.	11,100 sq. feet.

GORING PRIORY (Nuns).   A small church of chalk, rubble and flint, with Norman nave and Transitional north aisle having an arcade of three arches with circular piers, Norman western tower and a modern apsidal chancel.   There are a few traces of the conventual buildings.

OSNEY PRIORY.   There are some remains, though only slight, of this famous priory, on an island in the Thames.

OXFORD CATHEDRAL.   Formerly the Priory of St. Frideswide.   This, the smallest of our ancient cathedrals, is a building of considerable and distinctive interest.   The choir, and what remains of the nave, are Late Norman of unusual design.   Each pier has two half-capitals.   One supports the arch in the aisle; the other, at an appreciably higher elevation, supports the main arcade.   The triforium openings are between the main or upper arch, and aisle or lower arch.   The church as it now stands consists of choir with aisles, transepts, chapels and the eastern half of the original nave. The western bays were removed by Wolsey when he dissolved the priory and founded the present college.

The eastern half of the cloister remains, with its fine E.E. chapter house and its Norman doorway. It is a rectangular building.

The choir has a very beautiful and elaborate lierne vault, with pendants. The existing east wall is by Gilbert Scott.

The church serves the double purpose of cathedral and Christ Church College Chapel.

The styles are:

NORMAN	Nave.
	Choir.
	Transepts.
	Chapter house door.
	St. Lucy's Chapel.
EARLY ENGLISH	Lady chapel.
	Chapter house.
	Tower and spire.
DECORATED	Latin chapel.
	Some windows.
PERPENDICULAR	Cloisters.
	Choir vault.
	Windows.
19TH CENTURY	East wall of choir (Scott).
	Reredos (Bodley).

Total length	175 feet.
West wall to east window . . .	165 ,,
Length of nave	50 ,,
Width of nave	52 ,,
Width across transept . . .	104 ,,
Extreme width	108 ,,
Height of spire	144 ,,
Area	11,400 sq. feet.

WROXTON PRIORY. Some portions are included in the residence called " Wroxton Abbey ", and consist mainly of a few rough E.E. arches in the basement.

Gilbertine

CLATTERCOTE PRIORY. Portions of the conventual buildings (E.E.), chiefly vaulted chambers, are incorporated in a farmhouse.

Friars

Austin Friars

OXFORD. Gateway.

Rutland

Canons

Augustinian

BROOKE PRIORY.   Slight remains, incorporated in farm buildings.

Shropshire

Monks

Benedictine

ALBERBURY PRIORY.   Appreciable remains in a farm called " White Abbey ".   It was a Grandmontine house.

BROMFIELD PRIORY (c. Gloucester).   The present parish church consists of a portion of the priory church, namely a small Norman, E.E. and Dec. nave and north aisle (or chapel), with a fine 13th-century western tower.   Choir, transepts and conventual buildings are destroyed, though there are some slight remains of a later house to the south of the church.   There is a very good gatehouse.

MORVILLE PRIORY (c. Shrewsbury).   There is a small Late Norman church consisting of chancel, nave with two aisles and a plain western tower.   As the priory stood where Morville Hall now stands, it is doubtful if this was actually the priory church, though it probably belonged to it and was always the parish church.   There are no other remains.

SHREWSBURY ABBEY (Mitred).   The nave of the abbey church still remains (123 feet in length), the eastern half of which is Norman and the western Perp.   The Norman portion has a glazed triforium and a modern clerestory in Norman style.   There is an engaged western tower with a large Perp. west window.   The present chancel, nave clerestory, north and south transept walls (transepts are gone) are modern, by Pearson.

The only other fragment remaining is the reader's pulpit formerly in the refectory, which is still *in situ* on the other side of the road. This road passes over the site of the cloister.

Cluniac

CHURCH PREEN PRIORY.   A very small chapel—69 feet by 12½ feet—
is said to be the chapel of a small house which was a cell to Wenlock.

WENLOCK PRIORY.   There are considerable remains of great beauty
of this once-powerful monastery.   Of the church, part of the north
transept, most of the south transept, and the western part of the south
nave aisle, are still standing.   These are good E.E.   The three
arches of the Late Norman chapter house also exist, with its north
and south walls.   The remaining sides of the cloister are bounded
by the walls of the refectory to the south and the dormitory to the
west.   The Prior's Lodging is the seat of the Gaskell family, and
retains its original appearance to a remarkable extent.
   The house, ruins, cloister and gardens are beautifully kept.

Cistercian

BOSCOBEL, or BREWOOD PRIORY (Nuns).   Usually called " White
Ladies ".   There is not a great deal left, the principal relic being the
church walls, with a Norman doorway on either side.   It adjoins
Boscobel House.

BUILDWAS ABBEY.   A large part of the church is still standing, and
includes the west wall, both arcades, the crossing and the presbytery.
It is a noble piece of early Transitional work, with preponderating
Norman characteristics, and only slightly pointed arches.   The
chapter house and slype also remain.   The abbot's house, much
modernised, is a private residence.   Of the other buildings only
foundations remain.   The ruins are in charge of the Office of
Works.

Canons

Augustinian

CHIRBURY PRIORY.   Early English nave and western tower.   It is
of five bays, with two aisles; south arcade considerably out of the
vertical.   The existing sanctuary is a poor brick affair.   The tower
is the best feature of this church.   No other remains.

HAUGHMOND ABBEY.   Ruin (Office of Works).   Nothing is left
of the church, but there are considerable remains of the very beautiful
Late Norman chapter house, cloister, infirmary, Abbot's Lodging
and kitchen.   This is decidedly the most attractive of Augustinian
ruins.

LILLESHALL ABBEY.   Ruin.   A large part of the aisleless church is
still standing, the most notable feature being a fine round-arched
E.E. doorway in the west front.   Some portions of the monastic
G

buildings also remain, notably the refectory, but the chapter house has gone.   There is a good Norman door leading from the cloister into the church.

WOMBRIDGE PRIORY.   There are some slight remains in a private garden near the church.

Somerset

Monks

Benedictine

BATH ABBEY.   The existing church is very late, dating from *c.* 1500. It was left incomplete at the Dissolution, and not finally roofed until 1604–10.   It is therefore the last building of any importance during the medieval period.   The arcades are of the normal four-centred Tudor type, with a vast clerestory over.   The tower windows, also the east window, are square-headed, though the customary pointed head is suggested in the east window by heavy tracery.   The church is fan-vaulted throughout, though that of the nave is modern—by Gilbert Scott.

Bath in the 12th century was the seat of the bishopric subsequently domiciled at Wells.   The titles were merged in the middle of the 12th century.

There are no remains of any of the monastic buildings.

Total length	225 feet.
Height of nave	75 ,,
Width of nave	72 ,,
Width across transept . . .	124 ,,
Height of tower	162 ,,
Area . . . . . 15,220 sq. feet.	

DUNSTER PRIORY (c. Bath).   The church still remains as the parish church, which its nave always was.   It is a large building, mainly Perp., with neither triforium nor clerestory.   There is a splendid screen across the whole width.   The western door is Norman, much restored, and the short eastern arm, or chancel, is partly a reconstruction by Street in E.E. style, and is the property of the Luttrell family.   The fine central tower is Perp., 100 feet in height.

The parish altar stands under the eastern tower arch, in approximately its ancient position, while the priory chapel is furnished after the style of a small monastic choir, and is very interesting on that account.

There is a curious shouldered arch in the south transept.

The priory barn and dovecot (a very good example) also remain, and portions of the Prior's Lodging are included in some cottages, whose gardens occupy the western part of the garth.

Total length of the church   .   .   .   180 feet.
Height of tower   100   „

GLASTONBURY ABBEY (Mitred).   The legendary and historical associations of Glastonbury cause it to rank with Canterbury as the most sacred place in England.

Legend says that St. Joseph of Arimathea was a Phœnician trader, and the uncle of Our Lord.   He used to come here on his voyages to Cornwall (then a much larger kingdom than the present county), and on one of these occasions Our Lord, then a boy, accompanied him.   A well by which He sat, and in whose depths the Holy Grail was hidden at a later date, may be seen in the garden of a girls' school at the foot of the Tor.   After the Ascension St. Joseph with a band of companions settled permanently on the abbey site, building their chapel and homes of wattles and daub where the lovely chapel of St. Joseph now stands.   The story is well known of their landing on Weary All Hill on Christmas Day (for then the flat meadows between the Isle of Avalon and the sea were fen country and covered by the sea at high tide), and that he stuck his staff in the ground, when it miraculously took root and blossomed. Thus the first " Glastonbury thorn " came into existence, though it is not there now, having been destroyed by a Cromwellian soldier bent on extirpating " superstition ".   Every Christmas day the thorn blossomed, and an offshoot from it now in the abbey precincts does so to this day.

In later times the Isle of Avalon became the focal point of Arthurian legend, and the reputed graves of Arthur and Guinevere are to be seen in the abbey.

Actual history begins with the founding of the monastery by King Ina (688–726), its most celebrated abbot in Saxon times being St. Dunstan, afterwards Archbishop of Canterbury.   With the coming of the Normans there was much rebuilding, and nothing is left of the Saxon monastery.

The oldest part of the existing remains is the Chapel of Our Lady, or, alternatively, the Chapel of St. Joseph, which dates from the close of the 12th century.   It is the most beautiful building of its period in England, and occupies the supposed site of St. Joseph's wattle chapel at the extreme west end of the abbey church.   It is a richly ornamented rectangular building, and had a hipped roof, all four of its walls being of equal height, with no gable ends.   At each corner rose a turret surmounted by a low pyramidal spire, two of which still remain. The beautiful north door and the western wall with its three windows should also be noted.

The great abbey church lies to the east of this chapel, and was at first separated from it, but in the 13th century the two were joined by an intervening Galilee, the E.E. nature of which is clearly apparent.

The abbey church was more or less in continual process of erection and enlargement throughout the succeeding centuries of the medieval period. The remains of it consist of the E.E. western entrance from the Galilee, parts of the nave walls, a considerable portion of the crossing and transepts, with much of the choir and presbytery walls. All this work is of various periods, but a remarkable feature is the persistence of the chevron moulding (or zig-zag) which is normally confined to Norman work. Possibly the underlying idea was to demonstrate its kinship with the Chapel of St. Joseph.

Both nave and choir have lancet windows, those of the nave being the earlier; some traces of Dec. work may be seen in the nave, and some Perp. panels in the choir. The two easternmost bays of the choir are Late Dec., while at the extreme east end of the church are the foundations of the Edgar Chapel, erected in Tudor times. There are also the foundations of a little chapel opening off the west side of the north transept, which is said to be the Chapel of Our Lady of Loretto, and was the final addition to the fabric.

The foundations of the conventual buildings are also exposed, though the only actual building left standing is the splendid octagonal abbot's kitchen, now used as a museum. The gateway still serves as the principal entrance to the ruins.

Since the Church regained possession of this holy site some forty years ago, much excavation has been carried out, as the foregoing notes demonstrate. Doubtless further excavations will reveal still more details at present hidden.

MUCHELNEY ABBEY (Office of Works). The 15th-century abbot's house, with a part of the cloister and refectory, remain. Nothing is left of the church.

STOGURSEY PRIORY (c. Lonlay). A cruciform church, with a fine Norman aisled choir, transepts, central tower and late 15th-century unaisled nave which, however, retains its Norman west door. The tower is the oldest part of the building, and carries a later leaded spire. This priory was suppressed by Henry V, and the nave as it now stands was built temp. Henry VII.

The capitals of the Norman piers supporting the tower have some interesting carving. The choir has neither triforium nor clerestory.

Apart from the church, the dovecote is the only remaining feature.

REFECTORY (EXTERIOR) RIEVAULX ABBEY.

REFECTORY (INTERIOR) RIEVAULX ABBEY.

Facing page 92.

REFECTORY (EXTERIOR) CLEEVE ABBEY.

REFECTORY (INTERIOR) CLEEVE ABBEY.

Facing page 93.

Cluniac

MONTACUTE PRIORY.   The fine Tudor gatehouse is now a farm-house, and across a field the dovecote still stands.

Carthusian

HINTON PRIORY.   There is a curious building with chapel (E.E.) on ground floor, and library and dovecote over.   The refectory serves as an outhouse in the stable yard belonging to the present beautiful house called " Hinton Charterhouse ".   No other remains.

WITHAM PRIORY.   The small Lay Brothers' Chapel—a Norman building—is the parish church.   It is of three unaisled bays with eastern apse; the westernmost bay is modern.   The buttresses are unusually prominent.

It became the parish church in 1458.

The only other remaining building is the dovecote, adapted for use as the parish room.

Cistercian

CLEEVE ABBEY.   The remains are fairly extensive, and consist of the Perp. gatehouse and three sides of the cloister.   On the east side are the sacristy, library, chapter house, daystair, slype and parlour, with the dormitory over all; these are E.E.   On the south side is the refectory, chiefly Perp., and on the west is the undercroft of the lay quarters.   Nothing is left of the walks, and of the church only the foundations remain.

Secular

WELLS CATHEDRAL.   Though one of the smaller cathedrals, it is one of the most beautiful, with a superb west front (E.E.) containing an unrivalled collection of statuary, a fine grouping of three towers, and a charmingly grouped eastern arm, Lady chapel and chapter house.   The nave is E.E., not altogether free from traces of the Transitional period.   Its piers are exceptionally beautiful, with wonderfully carved capitals.   A unique feature is the continuous line of the triforium, stretching unbroken the whole length of the nave.   The vaulting shafts spring from corbels above the triforium, thus leaving the spandrels of the main arcade empty.   A very striking feature is the inverted arches strengthening the supports of the central tower.   The transept, also E.E., is double-aisled, with piers and carved capitals resembling those in the nave.

The choir arcade is of similar general character to those of the nave and transepts, though the triforium is altered to Dec. panelling. The presbytery is Late Dec., verging upon Perp., and is a very fine piece of work.   With the Dec. Lady chapel (which is five sides of an octagon, the other three sides with open arcades forming the retro-choir) this end of the cathedral is one of the most beautiful of medieval conceptions. There are glorious windows in both presbytery and Lady chapel.

The chapter house, lying to the north-east, is a splendid octagon with a central column, raised on a crypt of the same size and shape. The staircase leading to the chapter house is curious and ingenious.

There is a cloister on the south side of the nave, consisting of three walks only, there being no walk on its north side. It is of 15th-century date.

The Vicar's Close and the bishop's palace are two adjuncts of unusual character, the moated nature of the latter—though grim enough in its day—now adds to the charm of the cathedral surroundings.

The principal styles are:

EARLY ENGLISH   Nave.
                 Transepts.
                 Western bays of choir.
                 West front.
                 Undercroft of chapter house.

LATE DECORATED   Chapter house.
                 Lady chapel.
                 Presbytery.
                 Central tower.
                 Inverted arches strengthening the central tower
                     supports.

PERPENDICULAR   Western towers.
                 Cloisters.
                 Gateways.
                 Library.

The cathedral is vaulted throughout.

Mention should be made of the famous medieval clock in the north transept.

Total length	371 feet.
West wall to east window . .	315 ,,
Length of nave	161 ,,
Height of nave	67 ,,
Width of nave	70 ,,
Width across transept . .	135 ,,
Length of choir	103 ,,
Height of central tower . .	160 ,,
Height of western towers . .	130 ,,
Area	29,070 sq. feet.

Canons

Augustinian

BARLYNCH PRIORY.   Slight remains; now a farm.

BRUTON PRIORY.   The courthouse in the High Street (now offices) and the dovecot on a hilltop are all that is left.   This priory became an abbey in 1511.   Towards the close of the 15th century the priory rebuilt the parish church, the splendid nave of which is still so used. It is late Perp., and has a fine clerestory with niches between its windows.   The western tower is a particularly beautiful one, and is outstanding even in this county of glorious towers.   There is a second, though much smaller tower, over the north porch.   The present chancel, occupying part of the site of the monastic church, dates from *c.* 1743.

KEYNSHAM PRIORY.   Only slight remains.

STAVORDALE PRIORY.   A small foundation dating from 1440.   The church is converted into a private residence, with a modern wing to the north on the site of the east cloister range.   The nave retains much of its Perp. character, though the chancel is considerably altered.   There is no tower.

WOODSPRING PRIORY.   The church here is converted into a private residence, which incorporates also some portions of the conventual buildings.   The nave and tower are late Perp. (Tudor).   There were no transepts, and the chancel is destroyed.   There is a good gateway, some remains of the refectory, and a barn.

Staffordshire

Monks

Benedictine

FAIRWELL PRIORY (Nuns).   The chancel of the parish church, with Dec. and Perp. windows, was part of the convent church.   The rest of it, and all the other buildings, have been destroyed.

LAPLEY PRIORY (c. St. Remigius, Rheims).   This priory was suppressed by Henry V, like many other alien priories.   Most of the church stands, and is the parish church.   It has an unaisled nave and chancel, with a central tower.   The transepts have been destroyed. It is chiefly E.E., though somewhat featureless.   Its east window comprises five lancets, and there is a Norman window in the chancel. The tower rests on two Norman arches north and west, and one pointed arch east (restored); the south arch is walled up.

The upper stage of the tower is Perp.

There are some scanty remains of other buildings in the grounds of Lapley Hall.

TUTBURY PRIORY (c. St. Peter upon Dive, Normandy). The fine 12th-century Norman nave forms part of the parish church. It has massive piers, some of which are round, and some compound. The present clerestory is an adaptation of the original triforium, the clerestory proper having been destroyed. The south aisle is 14th century, and the north modern (1829). The chancel is by Street (1863–8).

The west front is Norman, and very good. It has a central doorway in seven orders, one of which is alabaster.

The tower, which is south-west, was rebuilt about the end of the 16th or early in the 17th century.

No remains of the monastic buildings.

Cistercian

CROXDEN ABBEY. Part of the 13th-century west front, with south aisle wall and south transept, still stand. Also remains of sacristy, chapter house, slype and parlour; and portions of the abbot's lodge and the guest house (Office of Works).

DIEULACRESSE ABBEY. Only slight remains, chiefly fragments of the choir.

HULTON ABBEY. Now called Milton. Foundations only.

Canons

Secular

LICHFIELD CATHEDRAL. Both externally and internally Lichfield is the most graceful of English cathedrals. Its three spires give it a unique distinction, while its fine west front and its apsidal eastern termination add greatly to its charm. Its modest height tends to enhance its length, and also to throw up the grace of the spires.

The nave is in the Geometric style, has an exquisite arcade of clustered shafts with foliated capitals, and a beautifully designed triforium and clerestory. The bays are divided by vaulting shafts (triple) which spring from the pavement to the vault without a break.

The choir is of later date, and is without triforium, but harmonises well with the older work.

Beyond the High Altar, the Lady chapel continues eastward with its vault at the same pitch as that of the choir, so that its apse forms the eastern termination of the main central avenue of the cathedral. The windows of this chapel are Dec., lofty and very beautiful, and contain some exceptionally fine old Flemish glass.

The chapter house is an irregular octagon, and lies to the north of the choir.

There are no cloisters.

The styles are:

EARLY ENGLISH   South transept.

GEOMETRIC   Nave.
Central tower.
Chapter house.

DECORATED   Choir.
Lady chapel.
West front.
Western spires.

PERPENDICULAR   Window and vault of south transept.
Other windows.
Minstrels' gallery.

17TH CENTURY   Central spire rebuilt (Wren).

19TH CENTURY   Reredos and screen (Scott and Kempe).

The cathedral is vaulted throughout.

Total length	370 feet.
Length of nave	140 ,,
Length of choir	112 ,,
Width of nave	68 ,,
Width across transept . . .	150 ,,
Height of nave	57 ,,
Height of central spire . . .	258 ,,
Height of western spires . . .	198 ,,
Area	27,720 sq. feet.

Augustinian

BASWICH PRIORY. Farm.   Wall with two Norman doorways chiefly, though there are numerous other fragments mixed up in farm buildings.

RANTON PRIORY.   Ruined Perp. tower and portions of the outer walls of the church only.

ROCESTER ABBEY.   Only a few mounds mark the site.

STAFFORD PRIORY (ST. THOMAS À BECKET).   The remains comprise a wall of the north transept, the base of the south walk of the cloister and part of the kitchen.

STONE PRIORY. A crypt in the house called "Priory House" and a few stones in the garden belonging to it are all that remain.

Friars

Franciscan

STAFFORD. There are some slight remains.

Suffolk

Monks

Benedictine

BUNGAY PRIORY (Nuns). The present Church of St. Mary is a Perp. nave, with no structural chancel. It is built of flint, and was erected by the parishioners in the 15th century on the site of a 12th-century conventual nave. It has a fine 15th-century south-west tower (flushwork), part of which, and part of the south aisle, was rebuilt *c.* 1700 after a fire.

The chancel, which was the nuns' chapel, is a ruin. It dates from *c.* 1300 and later, and is older than the present church.

BURY ST. EDMUNDS ABBEY (Mitred). All that remains of this once splendid abbey are an embattled 14th-century gatehouse, precinct walls, a bridge, two Perp. churches and a superb Norman gate tower. This latter now serves as the bell tower for the cathedral (one of the Perp. churches) adjoining it. There are some slight remains of the abbey church built into houses, and in their gardens. In the Botanic Gardens, occupying part of the site, are many fragmentary but interesting remains of other buildings.

EYE PRIORY (c. Bernay). There are only slight remains of this priory, though in the parish church the south chancel aisle (Perp.) is known as the "Abbey Chapel". Incidentally, this church has a fine west tower.

A residence stands on the site of the priory.

REDLINGFIELD PRIORY (Nuns). A small church of brick and flint of Norman origin, with Dec. and Perp. features. It was always the parish church, though used by the Nuns, and consists of chancel and nave (unaisled) and south porch. There are some scanty remains of the priory buildings, chiefly the refectory, now used as farm buildings.

RUMBURGH PRIORY. Remains; chiefly lower portion of E.E. tower. Farm.

SUDBURY PRIORY. Slight remains. The little church is now a barn.

Cluniac

MENDHAM PRIORY. Slight remains.

Cistercian

SIBTON ABBEY. Slight remains only, chiefly south wall of the church and the transept angle. There are also some remains of the refectory.

Canons

Augustinian

BLYTHBURGH PRIORY. Scanty remains.

BUTLEY PRIORY. Fine Dec. gatehouse, now the vicarage.

CAMPSEY PRIORY (Nuns). Some fair remains in farm buildings.

CHIPLEY PRIORY. Scanty remains, in farm buildings.

FLIXTON PRIORY (Nuns). Part of the chapel remains in a farm.

HERRINGFLEET, ST. OLAVE'S PRIORY. Ruin in charge of the Office of Works. Consists of the refectory undercroft (Dec.) and some outer buildings in a farmhouse.

IPSWICH PRIORY. Perp. gateway only, at a corner of the church-yard.

IXWORTH PRIORY. Residence, incorporating portions of the priory buildings, principally the crypt of the prior's house.

KERSEY PRIORY. The remains of this small house consist chiefly of portions of the church; two bays of south choir aisle with arches; fragments of tower, transept and west wall of nave. In grounds of private house called " Kersey Priory " and used as farm buildings.

LETHERINGHAM PRIORY (c. Ipswich). The parish church is the nave of the priory church. It is a small unaisled Dec. building of flint, with a Norman south door. It has a good flushwork western tower, but the chancel has gone. There are some remains of a 14th-century brick gatehouse and some carved stones at a farm called " Letheringham Abbey ".

SNAPE PRIORY. Scanty remains of a small establishment.

Premonstratensian

LEISTON ABBEY. Ruin, including choir and transept (14th century) and portions of the refectory and abbot's house; also an octagonal tower on the west side of the garth.

Friars

Franciscan

DUNWICH. Some picturesque remains; chiefly two doorways.

Dominican

BLYTHBURGH. Some remains.

SUDBURY. Slight remains.

Austin Friars

CLARE. Converted into a residence, and embodies a considerable portion of the cloister.

Surrey

Monks

Benedictine

CHERTSEY ABBEY. Slight remains, chiefly the foundations of the church and chapter house.

Cistercian

WAVERLEY ABBEY. The few slight remains consist of part of the transept, the lower part of the guest house, and a few other fragments. Chiefly E.E. There are two small outlying E.E. buildings also.
    This was the first Cistercian House in England, and was colonized from Aumone Abbey (Normandy).

Canons

Augustinian

MERTON PRIORY. Scanty remains, mainly foundations of the church.

NEWARK PRIORY, RIPLEY. Three bays of the choir, and the south transept (E.E.) are the only remaining features.

REIGATE PRIORY. Some E.E. remains in the residence of the same name.

READER'S PULPIT IN THE REFECTORY—
CHESTER CATHEDRAL.

Facing page 100.

UNDERCROFT—DURHAM CATHEDRAL.

CLOISTER GARTH—NORWICH CATHEDRAL.

Facing page 101.

Sussex

Monks

Benedictine

BATTLE ABBEY (Mitred). The existing buildings comprise the Dec. gateway, dormitory, E.E. refectory and the Perp. west cloister walk. Also some slight remains of the church. These buildings form part of a girls' school.

BOXGROVE PRIORY (c. Lessay, Normandy). The present parish church consists of the E.E. chancel (vaulted) and Norman low central tower of the priory church, together with the transepts and two bays of the nave (Norman). The rood screen forms the base of the present west wall.

Of the other parts of the priory, there are some remains of the nave, which had a north aisle with a pointed Transitional arcade; the Norman arches of the chapter house entrance; and the guest house.

A small, but very attractive priory.

Total length	120 feet.
Length of nave	20 ,,
Length of choir	80 ,,
Width of choir	48 ,,
Area	6,000 sq. feet.

EASEBOURNE PRIORY (Nuns). The east cloister range has been converted into the vicarage, and the refectory serves as parish room. No other remains.

RUSPER PRIORY (Nuns). Residence. Slight remains only.

WILMINGTON PRIORY. There is a 15th-century gateway, and a few other scanty remains, partly in a farmhouse.

Cluniac

LEWES PRIORY. This was the chief house of the Cluniacs in England. Only the foundations remain.

Cistercian

ROBERTSBRIDGE ABBEY. Only fragmentary remains in a farm, chiefly a crypt, part of the church, and an arch.

Canons

Secular

CHICHESTER CATHEDRAL. The main structure is Norman, including most of the west front, and the arcades and triforium of the nave and choir. The Transitional period is well represented by some first-class work in the retro-choir; while the vault, clerestory, vaulting shafts and some decorative shafts on the compound Norman piers, are E.E. There is a series of E.E. chapels to the north and south of the aisles which have the effect of making a five-aisled nave, in which respect it is unique among our old cathedrals.

There is an oddly shaped cloister to the south of the choir, but no chapter house.

An unusual feature is the belfry tower, which is completely detached from the cathedral itself.

The central tower and spire fell in the 19th century, and the present tower and spire are by Gilbert Scott.

The styles are distributed as follows:

NORMAN	South-west tower and part of west front.
	Ground arcade and triforium of nave and choir.
	Part of transepts.
	Western end of Lady chapel.
TRANSITIONAL	Retro-choir.
EARLY ENGLISH	Clerestory.
	Vault and vaulting shafts.
	Chapels.
GEOMETRIC	East end of Lady chapel.
DECORATED	South transept window.
PERPENDICULAR	Bell tower.
	Walls of choir.
	Cloisters.
MODERN	North-west tower.
	Central tower and spire.

The building is vaulted throughout.

Total length	393 feet.
West wall to east window . . .	295 ,,
Length of nave	155 ,,
Height of nave	61 ,,
Width of nave	90 ,,
Width across transept . . .	130 ,,
Length of choir	115 ,,
Height of spire	277 ,,
Area	28,000 sq. feet.

Augustinian

HARDHAM PRIORY. Some remains of the chapter house (Dec.) and refectory. Now a farm.

MICHELHAM PRIORY. Residence; incorporating a tower, prior's lodging, a crypt and the refectory. There is an eight-arched bridge over the moat.

SHULBREDE PRIORY. Residence; incorporating parts of the domestic buildings, called the Prior's Room and Monks' Room.

TORTINGTON PRIORY. Scanty remains (barn).

Premonstratensian

BAYHAM ABBEY. A picturesque ruin, consisting chiefly of the church and gatehouse; E.E.

DUREFORD ABBEY. Very slight remains of some arches in a farm.

OTHAM ABBEY. The canons who first settled here afterwards went to Bayham. A small 13th-century chapel still marks the site, and is now used as a barn.

Friars

Franciscan

CHICHESTER. The chancel, a 13th-century building with an east window of five lancets, is the Guildhall. It is situated in Priory Park.

WINCHELSEA. The chancel still exists, and is a plain Dec. building.

Austin Friars

RYE. The Late Dec. chapel is now the Church House.

Warwickshire

Monks

Benedictine

ALVECOT PRIORY. Farm; some remains, particularly a doorway inside the house.

COVENTRY PRIORY (Mitred). The only thing left is the base of one of the western towers, now forming part of a house. It lies to the north of Holy Trinity Church.

ST. MARY'S PRIORY, NUNEATON (Nuns). The present modern church of St. Mary is on the original foundations, and some lower courses and pier bases are incorporated. There are also some walls of the chapter house, refectory and dormitory, though slight. It was subject to Fontevrault Abbey, Anjou.

POLESWORTH ABBEY (Nuns). The parish church includes most of the Norman nave of the nuns' church. It has a north aisle and north porch, with a tower at the east end of the aisle. The western door is Dec. The chancel is modern (Street).

This church contains the only effigy of an abbess left in England. There is a partly timbered gatehouse.

WROXALL PRIORY (Nuns). The small 14th-century chapel, though privately owned, is used as the parish church. It has a 17th-century brick western tower, and is an aisleless building, with a Perp. east window, and three-light Dec. side windows. A plain interior.

The chapter house and refectory form part of the adjoining residence, which, however, has a rebuilt west front.

Carthusian

COVENTRY PRIORY. Vestiges only, to the south-east of the city.

Cistercian

COMBE ABBEY. Residence, incorporating north and west sides of the cloister (Perp.). The late Norman chapter house entrance also remains.

MEREVALE ABBEY. The chief building remaining here is the lovely Perp. gate chapel, now the parish church. Very little more than foundations remain of the rest of the buildings, though some walls still stand in a farm.

PINLEY PRIORY (Nuns). Some Norman work and a Perp. doorway remain in a residence called " Pinley Abbey ".

STONELEIGH ABBEY. Residence, which incorporates a few portions of the monastic buildings. The gatehouse and guest rooms (Dec.) are used as the estate office.

Canons

Augustinian

KENILWORTH ABBEY. The lower part of a 14th-century gateway still remains. The Norman doorway in the parish church is said to have been transferred from the priory church. This priory became an abbey very late in its history.

MAXSTOKE PRIORY. There are some ruins of the outer gateway and the central tower of the church, also part of the infirmary wall. The prior's lodging is now a farmhouse.

STUDLEY PRIORY. Slight remains.

Friars

Franciscan

COVENTRY.   The tower and spire of Christ Church were part of the friary church.   The rest of the present church is modern.

Carmelite

COVENTRY.   Part of the cloister is embodied in the Infirmary.

Austin Friars

ATHERSTONE.   The tower and chancel (Perp.) served as the Grammar School until 1888, but now form part of the parish church, with a modern nave.

Westmorland

Canons

Premonstratensian

SHAP ABBEY.   Ruin; the principal feature is a fine Perp. tower. Apart from this, the remains are scanty, though the plan is well defined.

Wiltshire

Monks

Benedictine

KINGTON ST. MICHAEL (Nuns).   Farm.   Chiefly the west range.

MALMESBURY ABBEY (Mitred).   Part of the nave forms the present parish church—a splendid Transitional building with cylindrical piers and slightly pointed arches, large triforium with four sub-divisions to each bay, and clerestory.   It has a fine stone lierne vault.

The east wall of the existing church is built within the Norman west arch of the former central tower.   The pulpitum forms the base of the wall.

H

The Norman south porch is one of the most celebrated and beautiful of its period.

Internal length is 95 feet.

The choir and transepts and the western bays of the nave are ruins, of which little remains. There are also traces of the cloister buildings.

Cluniac

MONKTON FARLEIGH PRIORY. Residence. The remains are chiefly of the refectory, and the foundations of the church.

Canons

Secular

SALISBURY CATHEDRAL. This cathedral differs from all the others in that it is in one style throughout (E.E.) and, though it lacks the interest and charm of succeeding styles, it undoubtedly gains in many ways through being " all in one piece ". Founded early in the 13th century on the removal of the See from Old Sarum, the building proceeded rapidly, and was finished in the main in about fifty years. Later additions there are in the strengthening arches of the tower, the upper stories of the tower, and the spire. But these do not detract from the uniformity of the church as a whole.

Externally it is one of the most satisfactory compositions of all our cathedrals. It has a fine west front, lofty central tower surmounted by the highest spire in the country, two pairs of transepts, and is a well-balanced design.

Internally, owing largely to the disappearance of its original colour schemes, it is somewhat cold. It is vaulted throughout, but as the shafts spring from the triforium, the spandrels of the main arcade are empty, and seem to call for some decorative treatment.

Each pier of the main arcade consists of a cylinder surrounded by four Purbeck marble shafts; indeed, almost all the shafts throughout the church—both in the main arcade and triforium—are of Purbeck marble. This, with the emptiness of the spandrels, emphasizes the horizontal line at the expense of the vertical. Nevertheless, the total effect is light and graceful.

The Lady chapel at the east end is unusual, having a double arcade.

On the south side of the church is a beautiful cloister, with a lovely octagonal chapter house off its east walk. The chapter house is built round a central pier, as at Wells and Westminster.

The chief styles are :

EARLY ENGLISH   The main building.

DECORATED   Two upper stories of tower.
Spire.

PERPENDICULAR Strengthening arches in north and south transepts. Flying buttresses of choir (south side).

19TH CENTURY Reredos (Gilbert Scott).

Total length	449 feet.
West wall to arcade behind altar . .	380 ,,
Length of nave	205 ,,
Height of nave	81 ,,
Width of nave	76 ,,
Width across transept . . .	206 ,,
Length of choir	151 ,,
Height of spire	404 ,,
Area	43,500 sq. feet.

Augustinian

IVYCHURCH PRIORY (ALDERBURY). Two Norman piers close to a cottage.

LACOCK ABBEY (Nuns). Residence. The church has entirely disappeared, but the mansion incorporates a considerable portion of the convent buildings, including sacristy, chapter house and parlour on the east, and the undercroft on west side. These are E.E. The cloister walks are Dec. and Perp., and in good preservation. On the north side, the refectory has been divided into several rooms.

Bonhommes

EDINGTON. This is the only remaining church in England of this Order, who had only one other (at Ashridge), which no longer exists. Little is known of them, but they seem to have been something between canons and friars. They were a late Order, and this " college " dates from 1352–61. It is in style between Late Dec. and Early Perp., is a cruciform building with central tower, and has a south porch like a smaller tower.

There are no remains apart from the church. The monastic buildings lay to the north.

Total length	154 feet.
Width across transept . . .	71½ ,,
Width of chancel	24 ,,
Height of tower	67 ,,

Gilbertine

MARLBOROUGH PRIORY. Remains very slight, and are built into cottages.

Premonstratensian

EASTON PRIORY. Foundations.

Worcestershire

Monks

Benedictine

EVESHAM ABBEY (Mitred).   All that remains is a fine detached Perp.
tower, forming the entrance to the present churchyard; an arch
(Dec.) of the chapter house vestibule; the almonry; and some small
portions of walling.   There are two fine Perp. parish churches.

GREAT MALVERN PRIORY (c. Westminster).   A splendid church,
178 feet in length and a width of 66 feet, with a beautiful Perp.
central tower 124 feet high.   The nave arcade is Norman, with
circular piers, and is surmounted by a large Perp. clerestory.   The
north transept and the choir are Perp.   The south transept has
gone.
   The gatehouse, alone of the monastic buildings, still remains,
though considerably altered and refaced.

LITTLE MALVERN PRIORY (c. Worcester).   The tower and chancel
(unaisled) are all that is left of the church, and now serve as the
parish church.
   It is mainly Perp., dating from *c.* 1482, though some Norman work
survives in the remains of the transepts.   There are slight remains of
other parts of the church outside the existing building, chiefly
fragments of the transept and nave.   The neighbouring residence
may incorporate the prior's house.

PERSHORE ABBEY.   The present splendid parish church consists of
the choir, south transept and central tower of the abbey church.
(Total length 126 feet.)
   The tower is Dec., and the south transept Norman.
   The choir is one of the most beautiful pieces of E.E. work existing.
Its piers are composed of clustered, foliated shafts, with beautifully
moulded arches; and while there is no triforium, there is a passage
at the base of the clerestory at triforium level.   The two easternmost
bays cant inwards towards a transverse arch in a quasi-apsidal
fashion, forming one of the most charming east ends in the country.
Originally the High Altar stood in front of this arch, and the Lady
chapel beyond it; but now the space before the arch is occupied
by the choir-stalls, and a small modern apsidal sanctuary has been
built to the east of it, occupying the western bay of the Lady chapel
site.   The vault dates from the second half of the 13th century, and
is a splendid example of its period (early lierne).
   The exterior is dominated by the fine Dec. tower.

LIBRARY (LEFT ARCH)—FURNESS ABBEY.

INFIRMARY—FURNESS ABBEY.

Facing page 108.

ENTRANCE TO ALMONRY—CANTERBURY.

ABBOT'S BRIDGE—BURY ST. EDMUNDS ABBEY.

The site of the nave and monastic buildings now forms a garden attached to " Abbey House " and belongs to the Anglican Benedictines. There are no appreciable remains.

Area of church 8,450 sq. feet.

WORCESTER CATHEDRAL. A cruciform building of moderate size, with a Dec. and Perp. central tower. The choir is a noble piece of E.E. work, with both triforium and clerestory; Purbeck marble is extensively used for shafts. The eastern wall is modern, and of E.E. design (by Gilbert Scott).

In the nave an extremely interesting feature is the Transitional work of the two westernmost bays, which constitute one of the finest examples of the period. The main body of the nave is later, the north side being Dec. and the south side Perp., although the latter is very close in design to its companion. Both sides are in the three stories—arcade, triforium and clerestory. The whole interior is very beautiful.

The cloisters are on the south side of the nave, and the chapter house lying off the east walk is circular internally (Norman) and polygonal externally (Perp.). It retains its original Norman circular pillar.

Of the rest of the monastic buildings, the refectory (Dec. with Norman undercroft) serves as Great Hall to the King's School, whose premises surround the former outer court. One of the gateways, called Edgar Tower, still gives entrance to this court. The Guesten Hall is a ruin, standing to the east of the chapter house. Dormitory and outbuildings have gone.

The styles are :

NORMAN	Crypt.
	Chapter house.
	Arches in north and south transepts.
TRANSITIONAL	Two western bays of nave.
EARLY ENGLISH	Choir and Lady chapel.
DECORATED	Seven bays of nave.
	Nave vault.
	Choir vault.
	Part of cloisters.
	Lower stage of tower.
	Refectory (King's School).
PERPENDICULAR	Windows in north transept.
	South side of nave.
	Part of cloisters.
	Upper stage of tower.
MODERN	East wall, with double tier of lancets.
	Reredos (Gilbert Scott).

The cathedral is vaulted throughout its entire length.

Total length	387 feet.
Length of nave	170 ,,
Length of choir	180 ,,
Width across transept	125 ,,
Width of nave	78 ,,
Height of nave	68 ,,
Height of tower	196 ,,
Area	33,200 sq. feet.

Cluniac

DUDLEY PRIORY. Some small portions of the church still stand, and apart from this only foundations remain. The eastern arm bears traces of Transitional work.

Cistercian

COOKHILL PRIORY (Nuns). Some part of the chapel walls still exist in the present 18th-century building.

Canons

Premonstratensian

HALESOWEN ABBEY. The ruins of this abbey belong to a farm, and are chiefly E.E. The barn on the north side of the cloister includes the south wall of the church with two doorways, and the west wall of the transept. Parts of the south transept wall and the south and north walls of the presbytery, with some portions of the refectory and undercroft, and parts of what may have been the abbot's house, also remain.

Yorkshire

Monks

Benedictine

LASTINGHAM PRIORY (N.R.). Strictly speaking, this church was not a priory church. A party of monks from Whitby started to build a priory here, but only constructed the apse, chancel, crypt, and lower part of what was intended to be a central tower. The work was then abandoned (1088) and the monks went to York, where they founded St. Mary's Abbey. At a later date this fragment was taken over as the parish church, the tower base converted into the present nave, and its Norman arches sub-divided into two smaller E.E. arches with clerestory added. The small west tower was added in the 15th century, and the groined roof of the church only recently. No nave proper, nor any monastic buildings, were ever erected.

A very unusual and fascinating church.

MARRICK PRIORY (Nuns) (N.R.). The ruins of the chancel of the chapel may still be seen, though much overgrown with vegetation. The present derelict church dates only from 1811, though the unusual set of three E.E. arches across the chancel may be the arches of the chapter house, rebuilt in this position, or they may possibly be *in situ* and the present church built round them.

NUN MONKTON PRIORY (Nuns) (W.R.). The nuns' chapel remains as the parish church, with a rebuilt east end. It is a perfect gem of E.E. design, with a western tower or turret constructed inside the church, which is a small unaisled building.

The internal wall arcading (with a passage) is very beautiful. The west door is late Norman, with zig-zag ornament.

There are some glorious Burne-Jones windows.

No other part of the priory remains.

RICHMOND, ST. MARTIN'S PRIORY (N.R.). Part of the chapel, with Norman west doorway and Dec. windows, together with an isolated small Perp. tower, are used as farm buildings.

SELBY ABBEY (Mitred) (W.R.). This is a splendid church, and the only Benedictine abbey church remaining in use in the six northern counties. It has a unique nave, Norman at its eastern end, and becoming more pronouncedly Transitional as it goes westward. The piers are round, compound and clustered, according to their date, with round arches throughout. In general, each bay of the triforium conforms to the style of the arch below it, and a remarkable feature of it is the manner in which some of the arches are supported, i.e., by a circular pillar surrounded by eight shafts under one circular abacus. The clerestories on both sides are E.E., though of differing designs.

The choir is a beautiful example of Late Dec. in two stages, with a pierced balcony between. The east window, of seven lights, is of Flamboyant character, and contains a good deal of its original glass.

The great fire of 1906 destroyed the entire roof and everything else of an inflammable nature. The present roof is therefore new (1909) as also are the south transept, central tower and—still more recent—the western towers (1935).

Nothing is left of the monastic buildings.

The styles are :

NORMAN	Base of central tower.
	West window of north transept.
	Two easternmost bays of the nave.
TRANSITIONAL	The rest of the nave.
EARLY ENGLISH	Nave clerestories.
	Upper part of west front.
DECORATED	Choir, and east side of north transept.
PERPENDICULAR	Great window of north transept, and other windows.
20TH CENTURY	Upper stage of central tower.
	South transept.
	Roof.
	Western towers.
	Choir—wooden vault.
	Nave—wooden ceiling.

Total length	. . . .	300 feet.
Length of nave	. . . .	135 ,,
Width of nave	. . . .	58 ,,
Length of choir	. . . .	142 ,,
Width of choir	. . . .	60 ,,
Width across transept	. . .	115 ,,
Area	. . .	20,000 sq. feet.

WHITBY ABBEY (N.R.). Ruin (in charge of Office of Works). The existing remains are of the church only, and consist of a fine E.E. choir and north transept, and some Dec. walls of nave.

YEDDINGHAM PRIORY (Nuns) (N.R.). A portion of the south wall of the church remains, with an E.E. doorway.

YORK, HOLY TRINITY PRIORY (c. St. Martin, Tours). E.E. nave arcades only; triforium (if there was one) and clerestory destroyed; the arcades, which are supported on octagonal piers, are built up; there are no aisles, and the chancel is modern. Western tower.
No other remains.

YORK, ST. MARY'S ABBEY (Mitred). North wall and adjoining portions of the nave (Geometric) still stand, with one tower pier, and form a splendid fragment. Choir foundations are uncovered.

Cluniac

MONK BRETTON PRIORY (W.R.). Ruin in charge of the Office of Works. The remains include small portions of the church, as well as of the claustral buildings. The 15th-century gateway belongs to a farm, and is the most appreciable building left.

Carthusian

MOUNT GRACE PRIORY (N.R.). The considerable remains, including church, are Perp. The arrangements of a Carthusian monastery, in which each monk had his own cell, are seen better here than anywhere else in this country.

Cistercian

BYLAND ABBEY (N.R.). Extensive ruin (Office of Works). An appreciable portion of the outer walls of the church (Transitional and E.E.) is still standing, including most of the west front (E.E.), which had a large rose window. A considerable number of floor tiles are still *in situ*. There are also slight remains of the monastic buildings, and the ground plan is exposed.

A beautiful ruin.

ELLERTON PRIORY (Nuns) (N.R.). On the Swale about a mile below Marrick Priory, on the opposite bank. The remains are very scanty, mostly of the small chapel, with Perp. tower.

FOUNTAINS ABBEY (W.R.). In the year 1132 the prior and twelve monks of St. Mary's Abbey, York, being dissatisfied with the laxity prevailing there at that time, left their abbey, became Cistercians, and founded a new home in the valley of the Skell on land given to them by Thurstan, Archbishop of York. It was a wild and inhospitable spot, and their early struggles are set forth in the account written by Hugo, a monk of Kirkstall, early in the following century. Thus Fountains Abbey came into being, ultimately becoming one of the greatest of religious houses.

The nature of its surroundings has altered enormously with the passage of time, the abbey now being beautifully situated in the park of Studley Royal, and one of the most picturesque, as well as the most complete monastic ruin in the land. Large portions of all the buildings remain.

Of the church, the nave walls and arcades are still standing, and form one of the most impressive examples of Transitional work left. It is in true Cistercian style, dignified yet severe, and without triforium. The choir was rebuilt in the early 13th century, with an eastern transept similar to that at Durham, and like it, known as " Nine Altars ". The great east window was Perp., as also was the west window.

An unusual feature is the superb Perp. tower at the end of the north transept. Like many another piece of late building, it is contrary to the Cistercian Rule, but is a beautiful structure, and a prominent feature of the ruins.

The west range preserves the fine undercroft below the Lay Brothers' dormitory; and on the opposite side of the garth are the

Late Transitional arches of the chapter house entrance. They resemble those at Furness and Kirkstall.

The refectory is a fine E.E. room. The kitchen, dormitories, infirmary and other buildings are all discernible.

JERVAULX ABBEY (N.R.).   Ruin.   There is little of the church left apart from the foundations, though a complete altar still stands in the north transept.   There are considerable remains of the monastic buildings, mainly of a Transitional character.

KIRKLEES PRIORY (Nuns) (W.R.).   Some remains in farm buildings.

KIRKSTALL ABBEY (W.R.).   Ruin of considerable extent, chiefly Transitional.   The church is unusually perfect, and has a noble Transitional west front, and very fine arcades, with clustered piers and pointed arches.   The cloister is exceptionally well preserved, and the outer buildings fairly complete.   This abbey was a daughter house of Fountains, and has appreciable affinities with that abbey.

MEAUX ABBEY (E.R.).   Only some mounds and a few stones.

RIEVAULX ABBEY (N.R.).   Beautifully situated in the Rye Valley, this extensive and lovely ruin is " a thing of beauty, and a joy for ever ", and since the Office of Works took it in hand the site has been cleared, much being revealed which was formerly buried. The nave, of which the lower courses of the walls and the bases of the piers remain, was in severe Transitional style, and Sir Charles Peers affirms that it is the earliest large Cistercian nave still standing either in Britain or France.

It is, however, the choir and transepts—the greater part of which, including both arcades, still stands—which give the abbey its incomparable charm.   This part dates from about 1230, and is perhaps the most splendid achievement of the period in the country.   Each face of the piers carries five shafts instead of the usual three; the capitals are exquisitely moulded; the arches are nobly proportioned; the triforium and clerestory are singularly graceful, for though the triforium is contrary to the Cistercian Rule, their basic idea of purity of style informs the entire design.   The east wall has a fine group of lancets.

The refectory is another beautiful building, the design of its interior wall being a most graceful piece of E.E. work.

The chapter house was an aisled apsidal building of which only the foundations remain.   In the cloister, a small section of the arcade has been rebuilt from original material.   Like all else here, it is a beautiful design.

There are extensive remains of all the other monastic and domestic buildings : dormitory, infirmary, tannery, brewhouse, and so forth.

The abbey was founded in 1131, and settled by a community of monks from Clairvaux under direction from St. Bernard.   It is the only abbey in England which can claim that distinction.

Its most celebrated abbot was St. Aelred (1147–66), during whose abbacy the nave, the lower part of the transept walls and the east and west ranges of the cloister were built.

ROCHE ABBEY (W.R.). Ruin (in charge of the Office of Works). The principal relic is the transept (Transitional), and a gatehouse. The foundations of the rest are exposed.

ROSEDALE PRIORY (Nuns) (N.R.). A small piece of wall, with stair, is the only portion remaining.

SAWLEY ABBEY (W.R.). The remains here are mixed up with farm buildings, but careful examinations have been made. It was not a large house, and its church was, until almost the end, quite a small building. The choir was then greatly enlarged, and indeed was not finished when the abbey was dissolved. The nave, or what is left of it, is still very small. Most of the other buildings can be traced with a little patience.

SWINE PRIORY (Nuns) (E.R.). The church was originally a cruci- form building, of which the chancel was always the parish church, while the transepts and nave belonged to the convent.

The nuns' part was destroyed, but its foundations were recently excavated. The chancel (parish church) is Transitional and Dec. with two aisles; the piers are cylindrical and arches pointed. The western tower was built in the 18th century.

This was a most unusual arrangement from two points of view. In the first place, it is a rare, if not unique, occurrence for a Cistercian church to be shared with the parish; and secondly, where churches of other Orders were so shared, the convent had the eastern part and the parish the nave.

SYNINGTHWAITE PRIORY (Nuns) (W.R.). Farm; there is a good Transitional doorway.

WYKEHAM PRIORY (Nuns) (N.R.). Part of the north wall of the church still stands in Wykeham Park.

Canons

Secular

BEVERLEY MINSTER (E.R.). A large cruciform church, with two pairs of transepts, and two western towers. The choir and transepts are exceptionally beautiful E.E., the nave Dec., and the west front and east window Perp. The principal transept is double aisled.

It is a three-storied building throughout, the triforium being a blind double arcade of much beauty. Although the nave is later than the choir and transepts, it bears a general resemblance to the older part, and complete harmony exists between the two periods. Even the vault of the nave is quadripartite, as in the choir.

The vaulting shafts throughout the whole church spring from corbels in the main spandrels, and many of them—especially in the nave—are of great interest and beauty.

The screen and Percy shrine are exceptionally fine examples of Dec. work, and among the most celebrated in the country.

The west front, with splendid flanking towers, is Perp. The crossing tower does not rise above the roof-line.

The chapter house was to the north of the choir, but no longer exists, though the staircase leading to it is still in the north choir aisle.

Altogether, this is one of the finest Gothic buildings we have.

Total length	333 feet.
Length of nave	171 ,,
Height of nave	65 ,,
Width of nave	63 ,,
Length of transept	167 ,,
Height of towers	163 ,,
Area	29,600 sq. feet.

RIPON MINSTER (W.R.).   This is not a large building as cathedrals go, but it has some uncommon features of great interest.

It must be admitted that the external appearance suffers from the loss of the three spires, for without them the towers are low and lacking in importance. Furthermore, the west front (E.E.) is composed of rather mechanical panelling, although, belonging as it does to one of the best periods, it is by no means without charm. The flanking towers are contemporary, and a specially noteworthy feature is the triple entrance between them—a rare if not unique arrangement in this country.

Until the dawn of the 16th century the minster still preserved most of Archbishop Roger's beautiful Transitional work, but of his nave there are now only two bays at the west end, and one at the east. It is of unusual design, having a solid wall as its lowest division, a blind wall-arcade above it, and a clerestory over all. The only windows were in the clerestory, for there were no aisles until the 16th century. The greater part of the nave was rebuilt in the 16th century, and is of a lofty and spacious nature, and altogether far more dignified than its date would suggest.

More of Roger's Transitional work remains in the north transept, the north side of the central tower and the north side of the choir. The western arch of the tower also belongs to this period, but the south-west pier is an ugly affair consisting of a Perp. reconstruction as far as the capital, and there stopping short. The eastern tower arch is narrow, and Perp. throughout.

The choir has three bays of Transitional and three of Dec. on its

ABBOT'S HOUSE—HAUGHMOND ABBEY.

KITCHEN CHIMNEYS—HAUGHMOND ABBEY.

Facing page 116.

ABBOT'S KITCHEN—GLASTONBURY ABBEY.

TITHEBARN—GLASTONBURY ABBEY.

Facing page 117.

north side, with three Dec. and two Perp. on the south.   Part of the triforium is glazed, an uncommon feature which it shares with the choir of Ely.

The oldest part of the Minster above ground is the Norman crypt to the south of the choir, with the chapter house and vestry over, which may be older than Roger's work.

Before any of the structure above described existed, there was a Saxon church here, of which the crypt still remains.   It is usually attributed to St. Wilfrid c. 670, with whose crypt at Hexham it has much in common.   It is reputed to be the oldest chamber in England.

The styles are :

SAXON	Wilfrid's crypt.
NORMAN	Portions of vestry and its crypt.
TRANSITIONAL	Portions of nave.
	Three bays of choir.
	North transept.
	North piers of central tower.
EARLY ENGLISH	West front and western towers.
GEOMETRIC	Eastern bays of choir and east window.
PERPENDICULAR	Most of nave and south transept.
	Two bays of choir (south).
	South and east sides of central tower.

Nave and choir vaulted; transepts, wooden roof.

Total length	270 feet.
Length of choir	95 ,,
Length of nave	133 ,,
Height of nave	88 ,,
Width of nave	87 ,,
Height of central tower . . .	110 ,,
Width across transept . . .	126 ,,

Area . . . . 25,280 sq. feet.

YORK MINSTER.   In area and general scale, York is the largest of the cathedrals.   This is achieved, not only by its length, but also by breadth and height.

The history of the Minster starts in 627, when a wooden church was built by the side of a spring in which King Edwin was baptised by Paulinus.   This building was shortly afterwards superseded by a stone one commenced by Edwin and completed by his successor Oswald.   It is not clear whether this church lasted until the Conquest, or if a later and more imposing edifice had taken its

place during the prelacy of Archbishop Aelberht towards the end
of the 8th century, but whatever church occupied the site when the
Normans came was completely destroyed with the rest of the city
as a reprisal against the revolt of the North.

The first Norman Archbishop, Thomas of Bayeux, built a new
church which seems to have had a relatively short existence, for we
find that Archbishop Roger rebuilt the choir and crypt shortly
after the middle of the 12th century, and if his Transitional work at
Ripon is anything to go by, it must have been a splendid choir
indeed.   Nothing now remains of it, and only portions of his crypt.

The Minster as we know it was commenced early in the 13th
century by Archbishop Grey, who built the south transept (E.E.).
He evidently intended to vault this transept, for there is a set of
springers at a lower level than those which are used in connection
with the wooden vault actually constructed.   This was followed
shortly afterwards by the north transept (also E.E.) under Canon
John surnamed Romanus, the Treasurer of the Minster.   His work
is superior to that of Grey and includes the five great lancets (the
" Five Sisters ") with a second group of five smaller graduated
lancets over them, making up what is, all in all, one of the finest
achievements of the period in any cathedral.   Both north and south
transepts are double-aisled.

His son, Archbishop John Romanus, commenced the nave, most
of which is in the Geometric style, at the close of the 13th century.
The arcades are lofty, and the clerestory is composed of large
Geometric windows.   The space between, normally occupied by
the triforium, is taken up with downward extensions of the mullions
of the clerestory windows, forming a " blind " continuation of them,
and having a passage at the foot.   It is apparent, however, that
another hand completed the nave, for some of it is in the fully
developed Dec. style of the 14th century, notably the great west
window.

The chapter house, despite its Geometric windows, also dates from
the early 14th century.   It stands to the north of the choir, and is a
beautiful octagon without a central pier, its vault being a wooden
one.   It should be compared with that at Southwell.

The third quarter of the 14th century saw the building of the
Lady chapel by Archbishop Thoresby, followed by the demolition
of Archbishop Roger's choir and its rebuilding in the last quarter
of the century on similar lines to the Lady chapel.   This eastern arm
is Early Perp.

The choir screen was the last thing to be built.   In its vault is a
charming medallion of our Lady.

The central tower was re-cased with Perp. stonework early in the
15th century, and the two western towers built later in the same
century.

There is no gainsaying the fact that parts of the Minster are disappointing. The greatest weaknesses are the absence of stone vaulting (except in the aisles) and the adoption of wooden imitations. That in the nave is definitely poor, though the choir is better. The curious feeling of frustration one experiences in the nave is probably due chiefly to the feeble vaulting shafts—mere single shafts rising from floor to ceiling. Imagine a series of compound shafts like those of Canterbury or Winchester, crowned by a well-designed lierne stone vault!

The choir and Lady chapel are a great improvement on the nave, though they follow the same general scheme. But they express it in a fuller and bolder fashion. The shafts, for instance, are larger and of greater projection, there is not the same bareness, and the vault, though still wooden, is more dignified. It should be said here that the original vaults both of nave and choir were destroyed in two fires during the 19th century, but the reconstructions follow the designs of the originals.

Yet, despite technical shortcomings, there is unquestionably a sense of power, dignity and spaciousness that make the Minster fully worthy of its standing as the Metropolitan Church of the North.

The crypt is entered from the north choir aisle, and is more interesting than striking. The eastern portion of it was re-fashioned in Perp. times to support the High Altar, and a good deal of the old material was re-used. At this end is a well, which, to judge from its presence here at all, may have been the one at which Paulinus baptised King Edwin. Towards the west of the crypt is a curious walled-off portion, with triple walls of enormous thickness. The inner, or middle, of these sections of wall is the oldest, and was formerly thought to have formed part of the Saxon Minster, though informed opinion now credits it to Archbishop Thomas. The outer section of these walls is Archbishop Roger's work. A great deal of the crypt was filled in with earth when the choir was built, and much of it is still there.

The exterior appearance of the Minster is extremely impressive from most points of view, especially from the north-west. From that angle one sees not only the superb west front, but also the north transept with the " Five Sisters ", and the chapter house. It has to be confessed that the lack of height in the central tower detracts from an otherwise ideal grouping; if it were thirty feet higher the balance would gain immeasurably.

Perhaps the Minster's crowning glory is its wonderful old glass, of which it possesses more than all the other cathedrals put together. The " Five Sisters ", with their grisaille; the great Dec. west window; and the still greater Perp. east window, are celebrated for their beauty. The aisle and clerestory windows are scarcely less beautiful.

The styles are :

NORMAN	Crypt.
EARLY ENGLISH	Transepts.
DECORATED	West front.
	Nave.
	Chapter house.
PERPENDICULAR	Choir.
	Lady chapel.
	Towers.

Total length	486 feet.
Length of nave	215 ,,
Height of nave	99 ,,
Width of nave	104 ,,
Length of choir and Lady chapel . .	223 ,,
Height of choir	102 ,,
Height of central tower . . .	198 ,,
Height of western towers . . .	196 ,,
Width across transept . . .	220 ,,
Area	63,800 sq. feet.

Augustinian

BOLTON PRIORY (W.R.). Frequently but incorrectly known as Bolton Abbey. It stands in a charming situation at a curve of the Wharfe. The choir (unaisled) and transepts form an exceedingly picturesque ruin, lying a little above the river. They are Transitional to Dec., and are very attractive. The nave is still in use as the parish church, and is mostly E.E., with some Dec. windows. It has a north aisle separated from the nave by four arches—piers alternately octagonal and circular. The west front, a beautiful E.E. one, is unfortunately largely hidden by the lower stage of an incomplete Perp. tower, which forms a roofless approach to the west door. The existing east wall is built in the west arch of the former central tower, and its lower portion is the original rood screen.

Of the monastic buildings little exists but foundations, though they may be fully traced. The chapter house was octagonal, to the south of the choir. The cloister was small, its east walk consisting of transept and slype only.

The gatehouse now forms part of a residence belonging to the Duke of Devonshire, in whose grounds the priory stands.

BRIDLINGTON PRIORY (E.R.). The nave of the church, and one of the gatehouses, are all that remain of this once great establishment.

This nave is a noble building of ten bays, the north side E.E. and Geometric, the south side E.E., Dec. and Perp.   The north side is in three stories—arcade (E.E.), triforium and clerestory (Geometric)—though the triforium arches are now open to the aisle.   On the south side the seven most easterly bays of arcade are E.E., but the tracery of the clerestory windows, dating from the end of the 13th century (*c.* 1290), is carried down to the triforium level as in York nave.   The three most westerly bays are Perp.   The west front is chiefly Perp., with a good doorway and large window, the surrounding stonework being panelled.   The base of the north tower is E.E., but both towers above the height of the nave walls are modern (by Gilbert Scott), the south being in the Perp. style, and the north E.E. and Dec.

There is nothing above ground of the choir or transepts, nor of any of the conventual buildings, apart from one gateway, the upper portion of which is a rebuilding in brick.

The measurements of the existing church are:

Length	185 feet.
Width	68 „
Height	70 „
Area	12,500 sq. feet.

GUISBOROUGH PRIORY (N.R.).   There are considerable remains of a 12th-century gatehouse, and the splendid Early Dec. east wall of the church.   Very little, but what there is is good.

HEALAUGH PRIORY, TADCASTER (W.R.).   Scanty remains in two houses, mostly some Perp. windows, and two chimneys; also some oddments mixed up with farm buildings.

KIRKHAM PRIORY (E.R.).   The remains include a fine Dec. gateway, part of the cloister (notably the Lavatorium—E.E.) and fragments of the church—E.E.   The whole site has been excavated by the Office of Works, and the foundations exposed.   The site is a beautiful one.

NEWBURGH PRIORY (N.R.).   Residence, incorporating some slight portions of the original buildings.

Gilbertine

ELLERTON PRIORY (E.R.).   Slight remains; chiefly lower courses of the walls of the church.   The original church became extremely ruinous, and was taken down in early Victorian days, when the present uninteresting church took its place.

OLD MALTON PRIORY (N.R.).   The existing parish church is part of the priory church, and is the only Gilbertine church remaining.

I

It consists of six bays of the former nave without aisles or clerestory (which have been demolished), the west front, and south-west tower. The base of the north-west tower also forms part of the front. The present east wall stands two bays west of the former crossing, and has three lancets (modern). The west front is very good, and is of E.E. design generally, including the fine south-west tower, though the doorway is Transitional and the west window Perp. The north arcade is wholly within the church, though built up. The three most easterly bays are Transitional, with octagonal piers; the fourth has Perp. panelling; the fifth and sixth are Perp. The south arcade, also built up, has only part of the piers and arches within the church, part showing outside. The four easternmost bays have round, moulded arches on cylindrical piers; the remaining piers are clustered. The walls filling the arcades are pierced with small plain round-headed windows.

The triforium, now acting as clerestory, has round arches enclosing smaller pointed arches. Some are glazed, some filled in with masonry.

The former central tower, transepts and choir have completely disappeared, and there are only slight remains of the monastic buildings in neighbouring houses.

WATTON PRIORY (E.R.). The fine Prior's Lodging is a residence. Apart from this, there are no remains above ground, though the complete foundations have been traced, and the plan drawn.

Premonstratensian

COVERHAM ABBEY (N.R.). There are two bays (Dec.) of the nave and some portions of the wall of the north transept standing in the grounds of a residence, which itself is built from materials of the abbey and includes part of the gatehouse. A beautiful place.

EASBY ABBEY (N.R.). Ruin (Office of Works). Fairly extensive, with a fine Geometric refectory. Considerable remains of the E.E. Infirmary, west range and gatehouse (Dec.). Very little is left of the church.

EGGLESTONE ABBEY (N.R.). Ruin (Office of Works). The remains include a considerable portion of the church (Transitional, E.E. and Dec.), which has an unusual east window (E.E.) with plain vertical mullions and no tracery. There is a fine 15th-century tomb base to Sir Ralph Bowes. The rest of the ruins are of a slight character. The situation is very beautiful.

Friars

Franciscan

RICHMOND (N.R.).   The beautiful Perp. central tower is all that
remains.   It stands on the edge of a park, to which it seems intended
to form the main entrance, though it is generally closed—doubtless
with the object of preserving it from harm.

Dominican

BEVERLEY (E.R.).   Some portions of the buildings are embodied in
dwelling-houses.

Austin Friars

TICKHILL (E.R.).   Slight remains.

PROVINCE OF WALES

Anglesey

Canons

Augustinian

PENMON PRIORY. There is a small cruciform church still in use, with unaisled nave and chancel, south transept, and low central tower. North transept is destroyed. It is mainly Norman.

The west range is converted into a residence; the east range is destroyed; the refectory is traceable. The dovecot still serves its original purpose.

Brecknock

Monks

Benedictine

BRECON CATHEDRAL. Originally a Benedictine priory, and a cell to Battle Abbey. It is a fine cruciform church, with central tower 90 feet high. Choir and tower are E.E. Nave Dec. There is a dignified modern reredos, erected to the memory of the first Bishop (Dr. Bevan). The guest house and other portions of the buildings have been adapted for use as the Deanery, etc.

With the exception of St. David's, this is the finest church in Wales.

Total length	205 feet.
Length of nave	107 ,,
Width of nave	59 ,,
Width across transept . . .	104 ,,
Length of choir	63 ,,
Width of choir	29 ,,
Area	12,500 sq. feet.

Friars

Dominican

BRECON. The chancel of the church (E.E.) now forms the Chapel of Christ College. Little more than foundations and a wall remain of the nave.

Cardigan

Monks

Cistercian

STRATA FLORIDA ABBEY. Ruin (Office of Works). The only walls left standing are part of the west front, with an interesting doorway.

Carmarthen

Monks

Benedictine

KIDWELLY PRIORY (c. Sherborne). The church is still used as the parish church. It is cruciform, with a western tower and spire, and is in the Dec. style.

Cistercian

WHITLAND ABBEY. Residence. Some carved stones are the only relics.

Canons

Premonstratensian

TALLEY ABBEY. Ruin (Office of Works). The principal remnant is a portion of the 13th-century tower.

Carnarvon

Monks

Cistercian

MAENAN ABBEY.   Vestiges only.

Canons

Secular

BANGOR CATHEDRAL.   A cruciform church, mostly Perp., with a western and a central tower (low).   It is an unpretentious building.

Denbigh

Monks

Cistercian

VALLE CRUCIS ABBEY.   Ruin.   A good deal left of the church and chapter house, with other parts of the east range, chiefly the dormitory.   Mostly E.E.   The chapter house is complete, and a beautiful chamber.   This is the most attractive of the ruined monasteries of Wales, with the single exception of Tintern.

Canons

Secular

ST. ASAPH CATHEDRAL.   The smallest cathedral in Great Britain, being only 182 feet in length.   It is a cruciform building with a central tower. Choir E.E. Nave and tower Dec.   Choir is considerably restored.

Friars

Carmelite

DENBIGH.   Site only.

Flint

Monks

Cistercian

BASINGWERK ABBEY.   Ruin (Office of Works).   Fairly extensive, with parts of the church and the east range of the cloister.   The refectory is the best preserved building.   Chiefly E.E.

Glamorgan

Monks

Benedictine

EWENNY PRIORY (c. Gloucester).   The church as now standing consists of nave of four bays with one aisle, central tower, south transept and chancel.   It contains the best Norman work in Wales. The north aisle, north transept and the eastern chapels of the south transept were destroyed.   The present north aisle dates from 1896.   Of the monastic buildings, parts of the enclosure walls and the gatehouse are all that is left.   The general style of the place shows that it was built with an eye to defence.

Cistercian

MARGAM ABBEY.   The Late Norman nave has been restored and largely rebuilt, and is in use; the six western bays of its original arcades remain, and the west front has three Norman windows above a recessed door (also Norman).   The somewhat Italianate "restoration" of this front is not satisfactory.   A few fragments of the eastern part of the church, with portions of the common room and the infirmary undercroft, still remain (E.E.).   The finest of the ruins is the twelve-sided chapter house (E.E.).

NEATH ABBEY.   Ruin and gatehouse.   Some of the walls of the church remain, and part of the west range.   The chapter house has gone, but the dormitory undercroft still exists.

Canons

Secular

LLANDAFF CATHEDRAL. This church has neither transepts, porches nor central tower, but at the west end is both a tower and a spire. Internally, there is no triforium nor vault. A prominent feature is the splendid Norman arch behind the High Altar, similar to that at Hereford. There are examples of E.E., Dec. and Perp. work. The cathedral suffered heavily during the recent war.

Merioneth

Monks

Cistercian

CYMMER ABBEY. Ruin (Office of Works). There is a considerable portion of the church, Transitional and E.E., including parts of both nave and choir, of which the east wall, with three lancets, is the most notable feature; also the lower part of the west tower and the abbot's house. The plan of the cloister is uncovered. An interesting little ruin.

Monmouth

Monks

Benedictine

ABERGAVENNY PRIORY (c. St. Vincent, Le Mans). The present parish church includes the choir, transepts, chapels and central tower of the priory church, all of which are 14th century. There is a modern nave, with north aisle (1882). No other remains.

CHEPSTOW PRIORY (c. Cormeilles). Part of the Norman nave is included in the parish church. The aisles have been demolished and the arcades blocked up. The tower (west) is a rebuilding; the chancel and transepts are modern—the south good, the north in very debased style. No remains of any of the monastic buildings.

MONMOUTH PRIORY. The tower and spire (Dec.) of St. Mary's Church were part of the priory, though the main body of the church is modern. There is a Norman respond at the west end. The only other relic is "Geoffrey's Window"—an oriel (Perp.) in the nearby school. It was an alien priory, a cell of St. Florence, Saumur.

USK PRIORY (Nuns). The nave, aisle and central tower are in use as the parish church. The tower has Norman arches, the space beneath it forming the sanctuary. The body of the church is Late Dec. and Perp. The choir and transepts have been destroyed. Portions of the convent buildings are now a farm.

Cistercian

LLANTARNAM ABBEY. Residence. Only the gateway remains.

MAGOR PRIORY (c. Tintern). Some fragments remain by the parish church, which was itself considerably enlarged by the monks. It has an E.E. chancel, and Perp. nave and transepts.

PAR GRACE DIEU. A few remnants are embodied in a barn.

TINTERN ABBEY. One of the most beautiful of our monastic ruins, charmingly situated on the Wye. The principal relic is the church, a noble Geometric building in a good state of preservation, with its arcades (except north nave arcade), gables, and east and west windows, and most of its outer walls. Though dating from the middle of the 13th century, the Cistercian ideals are strictly carried out. There is no triforium, or any sort of ornamentation, its beauty being achieved solely by purity of line and a skilful balancing of all its parts.

The chapter house, refectory and other buildings are partially standing, and the whole plan is uncovered.

The abbey is in the care of the Office of Works.

Canons

Augustinian

LLANTHONY PRIORY. Fairly extensive remains, chiefly of the church and chapter house. The E.E. west front is good, and its south tower together with the partially rebuilt west range now forms the "Abbey Hotel". There is also a ruined gatehouse. A beautiful situation.

Pembroke

Monks

Benedictine

CALDEY PRIORY (c. St. Dogmell's). This was a small house. A little vaulted chapel is the chief relic.

ST. DOGMELLS PRIORY (c. Tiron). Ruin (Office of Works). West gable of church, north wall of nave and north transept, part of cloister wall and part of refectory and infirmary. E.E., Dec. and Perp.

PEMBROKE, ST. NICHOLAS PRIORY (or MONKTON PRIORY) (c. Seez). The church is still in use. It has a small Norman nave, tower, and a Dec. choir practically rebuilt in 1889. The prior's house is a farmhouse.

Canons

Secular

ST. DAVID'S CATHEDRAL. The largest and finest church in Wales. It has a Norman nave, with a Perp. wooden ceiling, and a beautiful Late Dec. screen. The choir of four bays is E.E., and the Lady chapel Perp.

The central tower has a gaunt aspect.

The ruins of the 14th-century Bishop's Palace adjoin the cathedral.

Augustinian

HAVERFORDWEST PRIORY. Ruin; chiefly E.E. transept and choir. It was an unaisled church.

Radnor

Monks

Cistercian

CWM HIR ABBEY. There are only foundations on the site itself, but shortly after the Dissolution the nave arcade—a very beautiful piece of E.E. work—was taken down and rebuilt in Llanidloes Parish Church, where it still remains.

ALPHABETICAL LIST

MONKS

FRIARS

APPENDICES

APPENDIX I

APSES

MANY of the larger buildings mentioned in this book have apsidal chapels; sometimes Lady chapels, sometimes transeptal chapels. These are usually formed by fenestrated walls, and many of them are beautiful examples of their kind. By far the grandest of this type of apse is that of the Lady chapel at Lichfield, for owing to the fact that the Lady chapel extends eastward from the presbytery at virtually the same height, its apse forms the eastern termination of the central avenue of the cathedral, in which respect it is unique.

Of the large arcaded apse with a processional path behind the arcade and the High Altar standing before it, there are only six examples remaining. They are as follows:

AUGUSTINIAN

St. Bartholomew's Priory. This is a very beautiful Late Norman example, with cylindrical piers and stilted arches. Above is a Triforium in the same style. The clerestory is Perp. This apse is largely a restoration, though it probably follows the original design.

BENEDICTINE

Canterbury Cathedral. This apse is a very beautiful example in the Transitional style throughout. It has a lofty arcade, each pier comprising twin cylindrical columns. The arches in the curve of the apse are pointed, while those forming the north and south arcades are round-headed. The triforium is in harmony with the arcade, and the windows of the clerestory are round-headed. Within the space formed by this apse the shrine of St. Thomas à Becket formerly stood, the High Altar being a little to the west of it.

Norwich Cathedral. This is a singularly noble example. The arcade and triforium each consist of compound piers with round arches having flat soffits, forming one of the most satisfactory pieces of Norman work in the whole of England. Above the triforium is an unusually lofty clerestory in Late Dec. style, with a magnificent lierne vault over all.

Peterborough Cathedral. This is a Norman apse throughout its three stories. As it now exists, the ground arcade consists of openings into the Perp. processional path beyond, which is, of course, of considerably later date. These openings are square-headed and filled in with Dec. tracery. The triforium and clerestory are both Norman, although there is Dec. tracery in their windows.

The bays from floor to ceiling are divided by strong clustered shafts which, however, do not support a vault, but a flat painted ceiling. This results in a composition which is not completely satisfactory, though the general effect is impressive.

Tewkesbury Abbey. The apse in this church is in Late Dec. style upon a Norman foundation. There is no triforium, but there is a clerestory passage. The arcade is supported on cylindrical piers, the capitals of which are divided into two parts; the half fronting the presbytery is considerably higher than that which supports the vault of the ambulatory. There is an elaborate and very beautiful lierne (star) vault, and much ancient glass in the clerestory windows. The ambulatory is flanked by a chevet of radiating chapels, of which the eastern (or Lady chapel) has been destroyed, though fortunately all the others remain.

Westminster Abbey. The eastern arm bears no resemblance to anything else in England, but is a fully developed French style of apse, with lofty ambulatory and a chevet of radiating chapels. Parallel examples are numerous in France; *cf.* Amiens, Rheims, Chartres and Paris.

Pershore Abbey. The eastern termination of the presbytery at Pershore, while not strictly an apse, is a very unusual arrangement with strong apsidal features. It might be described as an irregular three-sided apse of which the middle arch is considerably larger than the two lateral arches. The clerestory is not carried across the eastern arch, the space above that arch being occupied by a lofty triplet of lancets, now walled up. Formerly the High Altar stood in front of this arch, but it is now situated in a small sanctuary to the east of it—a modern erection on the site of the first bay of the former Lady chapel. This quasi-apse is one of the most beautiful eastern terminations in the country, and it would indeed be difficult to imagine anything more completely satisfying.

APPENDIX II

Monastic Buildings

THE most complete arrangement of the buildings normally associated with the cloister is to be found at Chester Cathedral, where the chapter house with its vestibule, the slype, daystair and parlour still remain in use on the eastern walk; the splendid refectory, complete with reader's pulpit, on the north; and the Norman undercroft on the west.

At Durham there is a complete range of buildings, though only the dormitory with its undercroft on the west side is original. The chapter house is largely a modern restoration in Norman style, and a 17th-century museum occupies the site of the refectory. The cloister itself is disappointing, in poor Perp. style " restored " in the 18th century.

At Worcester, Westminster and Oxford the refectories and/or dormitories are used by the school in the two former instances, and by Christ Church College in the latter. The only building remaining to the church in these places is the chapter house.

At Canterbury, Gloucester and Norwich the cloisters remain, with chapter houses at Canterbury and Gloucester. There are no claustral buildings remaining in Norwich.

At Bristol the east walk of the cloister still exists, with a very beautiful Norman chapter house and vestibule.

The foregoing are the only remaining monastic cloisters, but six minsters were provided with cloisters, though their purpose was chiefly ornamental. They were Chichester, Exeter, Hereford, Lincoln, Salisbury and Wells.

The normal position for the chapter house in a monastery was off the east walk of the cloister, and it was usually rectangular in plan, though occasionally, as at Durham, Norwich and Rievaulx, the eastern end was apsidal. Westminster, however, has an octagonal chapter house, and Worcester a round one, both with central piers.

The chapter house of a Minster is usually polygonal, and to the north of the choir. It occupies this position at Beverley, Lichfield, Lincoln, Southwell, Wells and York. That at Beverley no longer exists; those of Lichfield and Wells are octagons with central piers; those of Southwell and York octagons without central piers; while that at Lincoln is a decagon with a central pier.

At Salisbury and Exeter the chapter house occupies the same position as in a monastery, i.e., off the east walk of the cloister; the former being an octagon with a central pier, and the latter a rectangle (restored).

At Hereford the chapter house no longer exists, apart from foundations and the lower courses of some of the walls. It was a decagon, and off the east walk.

At Carlisle there are some remains of the chapter house, and the refectory now serves that purpose.

Little is left of the claustral buildings at Ely, Peterborough, Rochester, S. Albans, Tewkesbury and Winchester, such as there is being ruins, restored corners, or embodied in later buildings. Gateways remain at each of them.

At Sherborne parts of the abbot's house are incorporated in the school.

In several cathedrals and abbey churches the abbot's house or prior's house is now the Deanery.

Gatehouses remain at numerous establishments, even where all else has gone.

At some abbeys, where the church has been demolished, one of the other buildings has been adapted for use as the parish church. These are:—

Beaulieu Abbey	The Refectory.
Kirkstead Abbey	The Gate Chapel.
Merevale Abbey	The Gate Chapel.
Witham Priory	The Lay Brothers' Chapel.

The other existing churches which still have remains of their cloisters are:—

Augustinian	Bolton, Hexham and Lanercost Priories.
Benedictine	Binham, Boxgrove, Dunster, Hurley and Jarrow Priories; and Wymondham Abbey.
Cistercian	Margam Abbey.

APPENDIX III

Number of Religious Houses

Augustinian	193		*Friaries*	
Benedictine	230	Austin		33
Bonhommes	2	Carmelite		52
Carthusian	9	Dominican		58
Cistercian	111	Franciscan		64
Cluniac	33			
Gilbertine	25			
Premonstratensian	36			

APPENDIX IV

Chapter Houses

POLYGONAL

There were in all twenty-five polygonal chapter houses in England, and one in Wales. The majority of them were octagonal.

The following nine are all that remain:

	SECULAR	BENEDICTINE
Octagons	Lichfield	Westminster
	Manchester	
	Salisbury	
	Southwell	
	Wells	
	York	
Decagon	Lincoln	
Round		Worcester

The other seventeen are either in ruins, or have entirely disappeared. They were as follows:

	SECULAR	AUGUSTINIAN	PREM.	BENEDICTINE	CISTERCIAN
Hexagon				Romsey	
Octagons	Beverley	Bolton	Cockersand	Belvoir	Whalley
	Howden	Carlisle			
	Old S. Paul's	Thornton			
Decagons	Hereford	Bridlington		Evesham	
Dodecagons				Tavistock	Dore
					Margam
Round			Alnwick		

The chapter house at Cockersand belongs to the Dalton family, by whom it was used as a mausoleum for a time. Its outer walls are a modern reconstruction, the interior being E.E.

All other chapter houses were rectangular, though only nine of them still remain in use. They are:

BENEDICTINE	Birkenhead
	Canterbury
	Chester
	Durham (a modern reconstruction)
	Gloucester
AUGUSTINIAN	Bristol
	Oxford
SECULAR	Chester—St. John's
	Exeter

There are many others which form part of present-day residences, or remain in more or less ruined condition. A particularly beautiful example of a well-preserved ruin is the one at Haughmond Abbey (Augustinian), which is Late Norman.

APPENDIX V

CANOPIED STALLS

MOST of the cathedrals have sets of canopied stalls. The oldest is at Winchester, and is of Geometric style dating from the 13th century. The most elaborate Dec. set is at Lancaster Parish Church, which in all probability came from Cockersand Abbey.

The late 14th and 15th centuries are the best period, and the most magnificent sets are at Chester, Lincoln, Ripon and Manchester—Chester being the finest. Exeter and Beverley also are very fine, while other splendid sets are at Ely, Worcester, Wells and Hereford. Westminster and York have good modern work.

Cartmel Priory has a very unusual and beautiful set, the stalls themselves being 15th century and the upper work early 17th century (Flemish).

APPENDIX VI

MEDIEVAL HIGH VAULTS

4 = Quadripartite.
6 = Sexpartite.
T = Tierceron.
L = Lierne.
F = Fan.

AUGUSTINIAN

	NAVE	CHOIR	PRESBYTERY	TRANSEPT
Bristol		L	L	
Christchurch		L	L	
Portsmouth		4		
Southwark		4	4	

BENEDICTINE

	NAVE	CHOIR	PRESBYTERY	TRANSEPT
Bath		F	F	F
Blyth	4			
Boxgrove		4	4	
Canterbury	L	4	4	L
Chester		4	4	
Crowland	T			
Durham	4	4	4	4/6
Ely		L	T	
Gloucester	4	L	L	L
Malmesbury	L			
Milton		4	4	L
Norwich	L	L	L	L
Pershore		L	L	
Rochester		6	6	
St. Alban's		4 (wood)		
Sherborne	LF	LF	LF	
Tewkesbury	L	L	L	L
Westminster	T	T	4	4
Winchester	L	L	L	
Worcester	T	4	4	

CARTHUSIAN

	NAVE	CHOIR	PRESBYTERY	TRANSEPT
Witham	4	4		

CISTERCIAN

	NAVE	CHOIR	PRESBYTERY	TRANSEPT
Kirkstead	4			

MINSTERS	NAVE	CHOIR	PRESBYTERY	TRANSEPT
Beverley	4	4	4	4
Chichester	4	4	4	
Exeter	T	T	T	T
Hereford		4		4 (North)
				L (South)
Lichfield		T	T	T
Lincoln	T	Asymmetrical	T	6
Salisbury	4	4	4	4
Southwell		4	4	
Wells	4	L	L	4

APPENDIX VII

MEDIEVAL ALTAR SCREENS

13th Century. Lower portion of Lincoln; the upper part is 18th century.

14th Century. Beverley Minster.
Christchurch Priory.
Durham Cathedral.

15th Century. Milton Abbey.
St. Alban's Cathedral.
Winchester Cathedral.

16th Century. Chichester Cathedral (wooden).
Southwark Cathedral.

MODERN ALTAR SCREENS AND REREDOSES

King's Lynn Priory	(Bodley).
Oxford Cathedral	,,
Wymondham Abbey	(J. N. Comper).
Hereford Cathedral	(Cottingham, Jr.).
Bristol Cathedral	(J. L. Pearson).
Peterborough Cathedral	,,
Selby Abbey	(Peter Rendl of Oberammergau).
Chester Cathedral	(Salviati and Scott).
Westminster Abbey	,, ,,
Ely Cathedral	(Gilbert Scott).
Exeter Cathedral	,, ,,
Gloucester Cathedral	,, ,,
Lichfield Cathedral	,, ,,
Rochester Cathedral	,, ,,
Salisbury Cathedral	,, ,,
Worcester Cathedral	,, ,,

APPENDIX VIII

Screens

In the larger monastic churches it was customary to erect two screens, the more easterly one being known as the pulpitum and the westerly one as the rood screen. There is no fixed place in the church for these screens, but it was customary to erect the pulpitum across the east tower arch, thus forming an entrance into the choir proper. This screen is usually a very large stone one and frequently occupies the depth of the first bay of the eastern arm. It had one entrance in the centre and on its east side it supported the return stalls. Sometimes the organ was placed on top of this screen, and it was also the custom for the Epistle and Gospel to be sung from it on Great Festivals. Examples in stone still remain at Canterbury and Rochester, while at Norwich the existing choir screen is 15th-century work in its lower courses only, the upper part being modern. There is a wooden pulpitum at Hexham. The only other one of which I am aware is at Malmesbury, where, however, it was built under the western tower arch instead of the eastern as usual. It now forms the base of the existing east wall of Malmesbury Church and its doorway is blocked up. The screen, or pulpitum, at Gloucester is a modern work entirely.

Rood Screens

The normal position for the rood screen was across the nave at the first or second bay from the east. It carried the great rood, and against its western face was situated the nave altar used for services for the laity in the case of Benedictine and Augustinian churches, and for the conversi in the case of the Cistercians. The structure of rood screens was different from that of pulpita in that they had two doorways, one to the north and one to the south of the nave altar. There is only one such screen remaining in its original surroundings, namely at St. Albans. There are, however, rood screens still existing at Bolton, Dunstable, Binham, Davington, Wymondham and Boxgrove. In the first five of these places the rood screen forms the base of the present east wall and the two doorways are blocked up. At Boxgrove the reverse is the case, the rood screen forming the base of the existing west wall, the doorways being blocked up there also.

The use of screens in secular churches, from minsters down to small parish churches, was confined to one choir screen, which, in the case of the great minsters such as York, Beverley, Ripon, Southwell, Lincoln, Exeter and Wells, is built of stone very much like a monastic pulpitum; but in the lesser churches, whether collegiate or simply parochial, the screen was generally of wood. In most if not every case these screens carried the rood, but they had only one doorway in the centre. There is, for example, very little difference in essence between the wooden pulpitum at Hexham and the normal chancel screen one sees in large parish churches in the South-west, such as Dunster.

Although I have cited Dunster as an example of parish screens, this church is somewhat exceptional, as the nave and crossing were always the parish church, and the chancel served as the chapel for the priory. The principal function of the screen in this building was to separate the priory from the parish, and its present position is not where it originally stood. But it is an excellent example of the parish church type of screen—perhaps the best to be found in any monastic church.

APPENDIX IX

DOUBLE-AISLED TRANSEPTS

THIS is a somewhat rare feature in our churches, and among those treated in this book there are seven so appointed:

NORMAN	Ely.
	Winchester.
EARLY ENGLISH	Beverley.
	Wells.
	Westminster (North).
	York.
DECORATED	Chester (South).

The ruined church of Byland Abbey also had double-aisled transepts.

APPENDIX X

PRINCIPAL BUILDINGS (EXCLUDING CATHEDRALS)

	EXISTING CHURCHES	RUINS
AUGUSTINIAN	Bridlington	Colchester
	Brinkburn	Haughmond
	Cartmel	Kirkham
	Christchurch	Lilleshall
	Dorchester	Thornton
	Dunstable	
	Hexham	
	St. Bartholomew's	
	Waltham	
	Worksop	
BENEDICTINE	Bath	Crowland
	Malmesbury	Glastonbury
	Milton	Lindisfarne
	Pershore	Tynemouth
	Romsey	Whitby
	Selby	York, St. Mary
	Sherborne	
	Tewkesbury	
	Westminster	
CARTHUSIAN		Mount Grace
CISTERCIAN	Dore	Buildwas
	Margam	Byland
		Fountains
		Furness
		Kirkstall
		Rievaulx
		Tintern
CLUNIAC		Castle Acre
		Much Wenlock
PREMONSTRATENSIAN		Easby
		Egglestone
MINSTERS	Beverley	
	Chester—St. John's	

APPENDIX XI

RELATIVE AREAS OF THE LARGER CHURCHES

York Minster	63,800 sq. feet
Winchester Cathedral	53,480 ,,
Ely Cathedral	46,000 ,,
Westminster Abbey	46,000 ,,
Durham Cathedral	44,400 ,,
Lincoln Minster	44,400 ,,
Salisbury Cathedral	43,500 ,,
Canterbury Cathedral	43,200 ,,
Peterborough Cathedral	41,090 ,,
St. Albans Cathedral	40,000 ,,
Norwich Cathedral	34,800 ,,
Worcester Cathedral	33,200 ,,
Chester Cathedral	32,220 ,,
Gloucester Cathedral	30,600 ,,
Beverley Minster	29,600 ,,
Wells Cathedral	29,070 ,,
Exeter Cathedral	29,000 ,,
Chichester Cathedral	28,000 ,,
Lichfield Cathedral	27,720 ,,
Hereford Cathedral	26,320 ,,
Ripon Minster	25,280 ,,
Tewkesbury Abbey	25,110 ,,
Rochester Cathedral	23,300 ,,
Bristol Cathedral	22,500 ,,
Romsey Abbey	21,470 ,,
Southwell Minster	20,480 ,,
Selby Abbey	20,000 ,,
Christchurch Priory	18,300 ,,
Southwark Cathedral	17,250 ,,
Sherborne Abbey	15,930 ,,
Hexham Priory	15,900 ,,
Carlisle Cathedral	15,730 ,,
Bath Abbey	15,220 ,,
King's Lynn Priory	14,650 ,,
Cartmel Priory	12,920 ,,
Brecon Cathedral	12,500 ,,
Bridlington Priory	12,500 ,,
Great Malvern Priory	12,500 ,,
Oxford Cathedral	11,400 ,,
Dorchester Abbey	11,100 ,,
St. Bartholomew's Priory	10,000 ,,
Pershore Abbey	8,450 ,,
Dore Abbey	8,000 ,,

APPENDIX XII

THE following is a list of all the other places where abbeys, priories or friaries formerly existed and nothing now remains, so far as I have been able to ascertain. At a few of them there may still be some vestiges, and quite possibly some of the residences may incorporate portions of monastic buildings in their present structures.

MONKS

Benedictine

PLACE	COUNTY	NOTES
Alcester	Warwickshire	
Allerton Mauleverer	Yorks. (W.R.)	Alien
Amesbury (Nuns)	Wilts.	Residence
Arden (Nuns)	Yorks. (N.R.)	Residence
Armathwaite (Nuns)	Cumberland	
Athelney	Somerset	
Belvoir	Lincs.	Dovecote
Blackborough (Nuns)	Norfolk	
Bradwell	Bucks.	
Burton-on-Trent	Staffs.	
Cannington (Nuns)	Somerset	
Canterbury St. Sepulchre (Nuns)	Kent	
Cardigan	Cardiganshire	
Carisbrooke	Isle of Wight	
Chester St. Mary (Nuns)	Cheshire	
Clerkenwell (Nuns)	London	
Coquet Island	Northumberland	
Cowick	Devon.	
Earls Colne	Essex	
Ecclesfield	Yorks (W.R.)	Alien
Flamstead (Nuns)	Herts.	
Folkestone (Nuns)	Kent	
Fosse (Nuns)	Lincs.	
Grimsby (Nuns)	Lincs.	
Grosmont	Yorks. (N.R.)	Farm
Handale (Nuns)	Yorks. (N.R.)	
Heanwood (Nuns)	Warwickshire	
Hedington	Yorks. (E.R.)	
Hertford	Herts.	
Hinchingbrooke	Hunts.	Residence
Holystone (Nuns)	Northumberland	
Hoxne	Suffolk	
Hoyland	Yorks. (W.R.)	
Hunston	Lincs.	
Ivinghoe (Nuns)	Bucks.	

PLACE	COUNTY	NOTES
Kilburn	Middlesex (London)	
Lambley (Nuns)	Northumberland	
Little Marsh (Nuns)	Yorks. (W.R.)	
Lytham	Lancs.	
Lymbrook (Nuns)	Herefordshire	
Middlesbrough	Yorks. (N.R.)	
Newcastle (Nuns)	Northumberland	
Norwich Trinity	Norfolk	
Norwich St. Leonard's	Norfolk	
Nunburnholme (Nuns)	Yorks. (E.R.)	
Nunkeeling (Nuns)	Yorks. (E.R.)	
Oldbury	Worcestershire	
Penwortham	Lancs.	Residence
Polsloe (Nuns)	Devon.	Farm
Redbourn	Herts.	
St. Neots	Hunts.	
Sandtoft, Epworth (Nuns)	Lincs.	
Sele	Sussex	
Snelshall	Bucks.	
Sopwell, St. Albans (Nuns)	Herts.	
Stanfield (Nuns)	Lincs.	
Stanford	Northants.	
Stanley Park, Stroud	Glos.	
Swaffham Bulbeck (Nuns)	Cambridgeshire	
Thicket (Nuns)	Yorks.	Residence
Wallingwells (Nuns)	Notts.	
Wherwell (Nuns)	Hants.	Residence
Wilberfoss (Nuns)	Yorks. (E.R.)	
Wilton (Nuns)	Wilts.	Residence
Winchcombe (Mitred)	Glos.	
Winchester (Nuns)	Hants.	
Wix (Nuns)	Essex	
York All Saints	Yorks.	
York St. Clement's (Nuns)	Yorks.	

Cluniac

Arthington (Nuns)	Yorks. (W.R.)	
Clifford	Hereford.	
Daventry	Northants.	
Derby	Derby.	
Heacham	Norfolk	
Horkesley	Essex	
Kersal Moor	Lancs.	
Kerswell	Devon.	Residence
Malpas	Monmouthshire	
Melton Mowbray	Leics.	
Normansburgh	Norfolk	

PLACE	COUNTY	NOTES
Northampton	Northants.	
Pontefract	Yorks. (W.R.)	
Wangford	Suffolk	

Carthusian

Hull	Yorks. (E.R.)	
London Charterhouse	London	
Shapwick	Dorset	
Sheen (Richmond)	Surrey	

Cistercian

Baysdale (Nuns)	Yorks. (N.R.)	Residence
Biddlesden	Bucks.	
Blea Tarn	Westmorland	
Bordesley	Worcs.	
Bruern	Oxon.	
Cokehill (Nuns)	Worcs.	
Dunscroft in Hatfield	Yorks. (W.R.)	Cell to Rievaulx
Esholt	Yorks. (W.R.)	Residence
Farringdon	Berks.	
Garendon	Leics.	
Gokewell (Nuns)	Lincs.	
Greenfield (Nuns)	Lincs.	
Hampole (Nuns)	Yorks. (W.R.)	
Keldholme (Nuns)	Yorks. (N.R.)	Residence
Legbourne (Nuns)	Lincs.	Residence
Leighton Buzzard	Beds.	
Llanllear (Nuns)	Cardiganshire	Residence
Llanllugan (Nuns)	Montgomery	
London, Tower Hill	London	
London, St. James's	London	
Medmenham	Bucks.	Residence
Newnham	Devon.	
Nun Appleton (Nuns)	Yorks. (W.R.)	Residence
Nun Cotham (Nuns)	Lincs.	
Pipewell	Northants.	
Sewesley (Nuns)	Northants.	
Stanley, Chippenham	Wilts.	Farm
Stixwould (Nuns)	Lincs.	
Stratford	Essex (London)	
Swineshead	Lincs.	Farm
Vale Royal	Cheshire	Residence
Vaudey	Lincs.	
Wetherby	Yorks. (W.R.)	
Wintney (Winchfield) (Nuns)	Hants.	
Woburn	Beds.	Residence
Worcester (Nuns)	Worcs.	

CANONS
Augustinian

PLACE	COUNTY	NOTES
Aldbury	Surrey	
Arbury	Warwickshire	Residence
Bamburgh	Northumberland	
Barnwell	Cambridge	Streets
Berden	Essex	A well
Bradenstoke	Wilts.	Bodily removed
Breamore	Hants.	
Broomhill	Norfolk	
Caldwell	Beds.	
Calke	Derbyshire	Residence
Calwich	Staffs.	
Conishead	Lancs.	Institution
Darley	Derbyshire	Residence
Drax	Yorks. (W.R.)	
Elsham	Lincs.	
Ferriby, North	Yorks. (E.R.)	
Fiskerton	Notts.	
Haltemprice	Yorks. (E.R.)	
Hartland	Devon	Residence
Hastings	Sussex	
Hempton	Norfolk	
Horsley	Glos.	
Huntingdon	Hunts.	
Hyrst-in-Axholme	Lincs.	Residence
Ipswich, Holy Trinity	Suffolk	
Ivychurch	Wilts.	
Kirkby Bellars	Leics.	
Leigh, Modbury (Nuns)	Devon	
Little Leighs	Essex	
London, Trinity	London	
London, Sion College (Nuns)	London	
Maiden Bradley	Wilts.	Farm
Markby	Lincs.	
Marton	Yorks. (N.R.)	Farm
Missenden	Bucks.	Residence
Moxby (Nuns)	Yorks. (N.R.)	
Nocton	Lincs.	
Northampton, St. James	Northants.	
Nostell	Yorks. (W.R.)	Residence
Ratlinghope	Salop.	
Royston	Herts.	
Sandleford (Newbury)	Berks.	Residence
Shelford	Notts.	
Stonely	Hunts.	

PLACE	COUNTY	NOTES
Tandridge	Surrey	
Taunton	Somerset	? Barn
Tiptree	Essex	
Tockwith	Yorks. (E.R.)	
Tonbridge	Kent	
Trentham	Staffs.	
Warter	Yorks. (E.R.)	Residence
Warwick	Warwick	
Wellow	Lincs.	
West Ardsley	Yorks. (W.R.)	
Weybridge	Norfolk	
Woodbridge	Suffolk	
Wormesley	Hereford	
Wymondley, Little	Herts.	

Gilbertines

Alvingham	Lincs.	
Bolington	Lincs.	
Bridge End (Brigg)	Lincs.	
Catley	Lincs.	
Chesterton	Cambs.	
Fordham	Cambs.	
Hitchin	Herts.	
Lincoln St. Catherine	Lincs.	
North Ormsby	Lincs.	
Overton	Yorks. (N.R.)	
Shouldham	Norfolk	
Sixhills	Lincs.	
Tunstal	Lincs.	
York St. Andrew	Yorks.	

Premonstratensian

Broadholme (Nuns)	Notts.	
Croxton	Leics.	
Hagnaby	Lincs.	
Hornby	Lancs.	
Lavendon	Bucks.	
Newsham	Lincs.	
Sulby	Northants.	
Welbeck	Notts.	Residence
Wormegay	Norfolk	

Bonhommes

Ashridge	Bucks.	Residence

FRIARIES

Franciscan (Grey Friars)

Aylesbury (Bucks.)
Badwell (Suffolk)
Berwick-on-Tweed
Beverley
Bodmin (Cornwall)
Boston
Bridgnorth (Salop.)
Bridgwater (Somerset)
Bristol
Cambridge (site of Sidney Coll.)
Cardiff
Carlisle
Carmarthen
Chester
Colchester
Doncaster
Dorchester (Oxon.)
Exeter
Grantham
Greenwich
Grimsby
Hartlepool
Hereford
Ipswich
Lancaster
Leicester
Lewes
Lichfield
Llanfaes (Anglesey)
London
Maidstone
Newark
Newcastle-on-Tyne
Northampton
Norwich
Nottingham
Oxford
Plymouth
Pontefract
Preston
Richmond (Surrey)
Salisbury
Scarborough
Shrewsbury
Southampton
Stamford
Winchester
Worcester
York

Dominican (Black Friars)

Arundel
Bangor (Carnarvon)
Berwick-on-Tweed
Boston
Cambridge (site of Emmanuel College)
Cardiff
Carlisle
Chelmsford
Chester
Chichester
Derby
Doncaster
Dunstable (Beds.)
Dunwich (Suffolk)
Exeter
Guildford
Haverfordwest
Hull
Ipswich
Ilchester (Somerset)
King's Lynn
Lancaster
Langley (Herts)
Langley (Surrey)
Leicester
Lincoln
London
Newcastle (Staffs.)
Newport (Mon.)
Northampton
Oxford
Pontefract
Rhuddlan (Flint)

Salisbury
Scarborough
Shrewsbury
Stamford
Truro
Warwick
Wilton (Wilts.)

Winchelsea
Winchester
Worcester
Yarm (Yorks., N.R.)
Yarmouth
York

CARMELITE (WHITE FRIARS)

Appleby (Westmorland)
Berwick-on-Tweed
Blakeney (Glos.)
Bolton (Yorks., W.R.)
Boston
Bristol
Burnham (Bucks.)
Cambridge
Cardiff
Chester
Doncaster
Gloucester
Hitchin (Herts.)
Hull
Ipswich
King's Lynn
Lenton (Notts.)
Lincoln
London
Losenham (Kent)
Ludlow
Lyme Regis (Dorset)
Maldon (Essex)
Market Drayton (Salop)

Marlborough (Wilts.)
Newcastle-on-Tyne
Northallerton (Yorks., N.R.)
Northampton
Nottingham
Oxford
Plymouth
Pontefract
Richmond (Yorks., N.R.)
Ruthin (Denbigh)
Sandwich (Kent)
Scarborough
Seale (Kent)
Sheen (Surrey)
Shoreham (Sussex)
Shrewsbury
Stamford
Sutton (Yorks.)
Taunton
Warwick
Winchester
Yarmouth
York

AUSTIN FRIARS

Boston
Bristol
Droitwich
Gorleston (Suffolk)
Grimsby
Hull
Huntingdon
King's Lynn
Knaresboro' (Maturins)
Leicester
Lincoln
Ludlow (Salop.)
Newark

Newcastle-on-Tyne
Northallerton
Northampton
Norwich
Orford (Suffolk)
Penrith (Cumberland)
Shrewsbury
Stafford
Stamford
Warrington
Winchester
York

PRINTED IN GREAT BRITAIN BY RICHARD CLAY AND COMPANY, LTD.,
BUNGAY, SUFFOLK.